GETTING THE CONNECTIONS RIGHT

Other works in the series:

The New News v. The Old News:
The Press and Politics in the 1990s
Essays by Jay Rosen and Paul Taylor

Covering the World:
International Television News Services
Essay by Lewis A. Friedland

Reinventing the Newspaper
Essays by Frank Denton and Howard Kurtz

At What Price?
Libel Law and Freedom of the Press
Essays by Martin London and Barbara Dill

The Beat Goes On:
President Clinton's First Year with the Media
Essay by Tom Rosenstiel

1996 ◆ THE TWENTIETH CENTURY FUND PRESS ◆ NEW YORK

PERSPECTIVES
ON THE NEWS

GETTING THE CONNECTIONS RIGHT

Public Journalism and the Troubles in the Press

Jay Rosen

A Twentieth Century Fund Essay

Library of Congress Cataloging-in-Publication Data

Rosen, Jay, 1956–
   Getting the connections right : public journalism and the troubles in the press / Jay Rosen.
      p.   cm. -- (Perspectives on the news)
   Includes bibliographical references and index.
   ISBN 0-87078-385-8
   1. Journalism--Social aspects.   I. Title. II. Series.
PN4749.R665   1996
302.23'0973--dc20   96–1443

                                                                                        CIP

Cover design and illustration: Claude Goodwin
Manufactured in the United States of America.

FOREWORD

The American system of government and economics is dependent on a knowledgeable public. We believe that democracy cannot thrive unless voters understand the choices before them and the consequences of their actions. Successful capitalism, in a roughly parallel way, depends upon a flow of information that gives rational investors and consumers enough facts to make wise choices. We rely on an aggressively free market system of media to provide us with enough of both sorts of information. In practice, strong financial incentives underpin the production and dissemination of vast amounts of business and economic information. But, when it comes to public policy, there is considerable debate about whether or not the media market provides enough good, solid information to meet the needs of citizens.

Perhaps this result should not be surprising; the media business, like any other commercial enterprise, is most interested in maximizing profits. And with increasing competition within the industry, especially in television, there is bound to be pressure to curtail or alter any activity that does not produce large enough audiences to attract advertising dollars. It takes no special insight to recognize that entertainment, broadly conceived, appears to be the key to capturing large audiences and thus large revenues. Of course, it is true that news can sometimes be entertaining to some people (perhaps not always intentionally), and that there is even a market for serious news programming. Still, either scholars and many journalists themselves are all wrong, or there is a growing shortfall in the sort of information—objective, in-depth reporting and analysis—that the public needs to make informed decisions. Indeed, over the past several years, a number of Twentieth Century Fund authors and task force members have argued persuasively that most political news is reported in ways that encourage cynicism among voters and sloganeering by politicians. What is perhaps more ominous is that most observers believe that there is increasing pressure to reduce the existing level of serious news and public affairs programming.

In the pages that follow, Jay Rosen, professor of journalism at New York University, not only explores some of the important implications of these developments, but also offers a prescription that would make the media better able to serve our needs. Rosen draws a familiar distinction between the media business in which journalists work and the valuable product they produce, journalism. Reporters presumably have professional and personal goals (the truth, getting a good story, exposing fraud and abuse, writing well, and so forth) that are not identical with those of shareholders in communications companies. In many cases, like physicians and teachers, for example, journalists have an interest in going beyond what the market itself might demand of them.

Rosen advocates a strategy—"public journalism"—intended to meet both the standards of our better journalists and the needs of all citizens in a democracy. The movement for public journalism (or, as others term it, "civic journalism") springs from a conviction that something essential is being lost in the rapid transformation of the news business that is under way in the United States and around the globe.

Getting the Connections Right: Public Journalism and the Troubles in the Press is the latest in the Fund's Perspectives on the News series of essays. In an earlier volume, Jay Rosen joined Paul Taylor to analyze current trends in *The New News v. The Old News: The Press and Politics in the 1990s.* Other volumes in the series are *The Beat Goes On: President Clinton's First Year with the Media* by Tom Rosenstiel, *Reinventing the Newspaper* by Frank Denton and Howard Kurtz, *Covering the World: International Television News Services* by Lewis A. Friedland, and *At What Price? Libel Law and Freedom of the Press* by Martin London and Barbara Dill. Our past reports have examined such diverse issues as the effects of television on presidential elections (*Presidential Television* by Newton Minow, Lee Mitchell, and John Bartlow Martin), the problems of coverage of international events (*International News Services* by Jonathan Fenby), the relationship between government and the press (*Press Freedoms Under Pressure: The Report of the Task Force on the Government and the Press* and *A Free and Responsive Press: The Report of the Task Force for a National News Council*), and the issue of televised presidential debates (*Beyond Debate, For Great Debates,* and *A Proper Institution*). In addition, the

Fund is currently supporting examinations of television and the judiciary by Ronald Goldfarb and the forces influencing the media by Trudy Lieberman.

*   *   *

While to be truly free a press must be virtually unencumbered by public rules and regulations, that does not mean that only an unexamined press is worth having. Moreover, the very professionalism so treasured by members of the fourth estate must stand for more than simply what sells. At the very least, we can hope for an increase in peer pressure among journalists: more shame and guilt for the bad actors, and alternatively more approval and applause for those who cover the news responsibly. In this spirit, the Fund is committed to continuing support for provocative ideas about the press and democracy. Our aim is to encourage dialogue, not only between the press and the public, but among journalists who strive to create and define better ways to frame and report the news.

It is not uncommon in the media world to hold postmortems and lament the way the last campaign or controversy was covered. Such talk rarely produces much change. What Rosen suggests instead is for journalists to question how they think—to maintain their professional skepticism but to use it as a tool to make thoughtful judgments about how the news can be reported in a way that makes it a prime source of enlightened public discourse. On behalf of the Trustees of the Twentieth Century Fund, I thank him for this latest addition to our series.

RICHARD C. LEONE, PRESIDENT
The Twentieth Century Fund
January 1996

CONTENTS

INTRODUCTION

In 1970, the *New York Times* inaugurated its op-ed page. The idea was hardly new (it had been tried in the 1920s), but it was out of favor at nearly all newspapers. With the success of the *Times* page, others soon followed suit—and today it is impossible to imagine political dialogue without the exchange of ideas on all the similar pages around the country.

More than an improved product, the result of the *Times'* experiment was a tangible improvement in public life. The op-ed page added something to our daily capacity to make sense of the world, creating a new and highly visible forum where, with the help of able writers, we can work out our responses to public events. This too was journalism, but of a type we rarely contemplate. It does not report on events, or tell entertaining tales. The "journalism" involved in creating and maintaining the op-ed page does something different: it clears a space where the public can do its work.

That we need more of this kind of journalism—the kind that invites people to *become* a public—is the premise behind a small reform movement that has risen from the ranks of the American press. It is called "public journalism," or at times "civic journalism," and its aim is to experiment with the power of the daily press, just as the *Times* did to such impressive effect in 1970.

Public journalism calls on the press to help revive civic life and improve public dialogue—and to fashion a coherent response to the deepening troubles in our civic climate, most of which implicate journalists. At a time of grave doubts about the future of the press and broad concern about the health of American democracy, those involved see this as the hour for creative experiment and piecemeal reform, for frank discussion about ultimate aims and possible ends, for innovations as bold and lasting as the arrival of the op-ed page. By changing what they do and how they approach their task, those experimenting with public journalism have rediscovered the power of the

1

democratic ideal as an organizing principle for their work. Self-governance, public deliberation, participatory democracy—these familiar themes, if taken seriously, can recharge the batteries of the press and show the way to much-needed reforms.

As many in the press have come to realize, this is a moment of truth in American newsrooms.[1] No one knows whether "journalism," as presently done, can survive the commercial pressures of an expanded media universe. At the same time, there is no telling where the floating discontent with politics and public life will lead. One thing is clear, however: there can be no safe haven for journalists, no point outside the current mess from which they can observe what happens without themselves contributing—to the deepening problems, or to possible solutions.

Public journalism is thus a confrontation with a long-suppressed fact: the press is a participant in our national life. It suffers when the quality of public life erodes. And when the performance of the press deteriorates—as it has in recent years—then public life suffers as well. This means there are limits to the stance of the observer in journalism; but the American press has no philosophy that takes over when those limits are reached. Public journalism provides one.

In the words of James W. Carey, perhaps our most accomplished press scholar: "Journalists need to start telling themselves a different story."[2] As reporters detached from the scene, or as "watchdogs" standing guard over it, they have an effective tale to tell: they offer useful information and a check on power. But they lack a story that would make real to them, and acceptable to us, their equally-important role as actors in the drama of public life, people with a civic identity as well as a professional facade, players (of a sort) in the political game, men and women with a reciprocal influence on public life.

Robert MacNeil, the longtime host of the *MacNeil/Lehrer NewsHour* on PBS, put the argument soundly in a 1995 speech. "We have to remember, as journalists, that we may be observers but we are not totally disinterested observers," he said. "We are not social engineers, but each one of us has a stake in the health of this democracy. Democracy and the social contract that makes it work are held together by a delicate web of trust, and all of us in journalism hold edges of the web. We are not just amused bystanders, watching the idiots screw it up."[3]

Public journalism is grounded in Carey's call for a "different story" and MacNeil's conviction that journalists are "not just amused bystanders." Its primary claim is that the press can do more—much more than it has been doing—to engage people as citizens, to improve public discussion, to help communities solve problems, and to aid in the country's search for a workable public life. These assertions, which hardly sound radical, nonetheless collide with conventional thinking in journalism. The result has been some provocative headlines in the trade press.[4] But so far the debate has not moved beyond a superficial understanding of what the people who believe in this approach are doing and saying.

I am one of those people. Since 1990, I have been engaged in a campaign of persuasion, trying to get journalists to grapple with the ideas behind public journalism. At the same time I have collaborated with practitioners in an effort to clarify the term and discover what it means in practice. I have defended the emerging approach against the criticism it receives, some of it quite understandable. Public journalism, then, is something I am attempting to bring about, in partnership with professionals in the field, along with others in the academic and foundation worlds.

The following essay is an introduction to what public journalism is about and a statement of why it is needed. I believe the movement has something to say about the political moment and the predicament of the American press. In the pages that follow, I will explain what the message is. I will also reply to some of the common criticisms of public journalism, many of which stir up professional passions but fail to address its central claims.

*   *   *

The history of the press can be read as one chapter in a larger tale: what is often called the "American experiment." The term refers to our lengthy adventure in nationhood, grounded in nothing more mystical than the requirements of a constitutional democracy. The American experiment is a continuous political test, in the sense that there is no deeper footing than democracy, no state religion or revered monarchy, to hold the country together.

As a powerful institution that is part of the experiment, the press is itself continually tested. Like the rest of us, it may rise to the occasion or be found wanting. Part of the story the press tells itself concerns the direction from which a potent challenge is likely to come. In journalism's professional lore, the government is seen as the primary antagonist and the First Amendment as the source of protection. But today the strongest challenge is not an imperial presidency or an intrusive government. It is changes in the broader culture that undermine public life, weaken the demand for good journalism and compel a serious response.

In explaining his decision in August 1995 to retire from the U.S. Senate, Bill Bradley said he had come to the conclusion that "the dialogue that we were having in the political process was fundamentally disconnected" from the lives of most Americans.[5] Bradley's is only one voice in a many-sided conversation concerning our collapsing faith in politics and what might be done about it. In *Why Americans Hate Politics*, journalist E. J. Dionne of the *Washington Post* pointed to the "false choices" framed by a tiresome and rancorous debate between liberals and conservatives. Politics, he said, is failing citizens as citizens withdraw from politics.[6]

This was also the conclusion of a much-cited study by the Harwood Group published in 1991 by the Kettering Foundation. As David Mathews, president of the foundation, wrote in introducing the report,

> People know exactly who dislodged them from their rightful place in American democracy. They point the finger at politi-cians, at powerful lobbyists, and—this came as a surprise— at people in the media. They see these groups as a political class, the rulers of an oligarchy that has replaced democracy. Unlike political scientists, however, citizens do not regard this as an "objective reality" and, inevitably, they are hop-ping mad about the situation![7]

Not only are the political system and the media establishment a source of deep frustration, but public life is faltering in many of its broader dimensions. According to research by scholar Robert Putnam, Americans have grown less and less engaged in communal activities. Participation in all manner of civic associations—PTAs, neighborhood groups, even bowling leagues—has suffered a long-term decline.[8] Suspicious and resentful of large institutions, citizens are also becom-ing strangers to one another as they interact less often in public set-tings. Perhaps the starkest symbol of this pattern is the rise of so-called private communities, walled off from the rest of society by security guards and iron gates.[9]

Over time these trends do more than busy the phone lines at radio call-in shows. They wear away at the bonds of trust, the habits of mind and heart, that ultimately make for a democratic society. What one author calls "democratic dispositions" are difficult to sustain in a deep-ening climate of suspicion and withdrawal.[10] This is the cultural chal-lenge contained within America's political experiment: Can we maintain the kind of civic climate that gives democratic politics a chance to do its work?

Journalists have a more than a passing interest in this question, although it is sometimes hard for them to see it. They are currently undergoing their own ordeal as resentment against the press builds while commercial pressures intensify. Newsrooms were once a haven from market forces; now they have lost that protection.[11] Worried about survival in a shifting media landscape, journalists confront at the same time the obsolescence of many ingrained attitudes and daily habits.

Since the era of Vietnam and Watergate, the press has regarded itself as our demystifer-in-chief. It has cultivated a way of seeing that sees through the facades that typify politics in the media age.[12] But with politics becoming more and more demystified, and with trust in all institutions reaching dangerous lows, the press needs to find a new way of seeing—not less skeptical but more useful for a society that needs to learn again how to discuss issues and solve problems. This is part of what Carey means by a "different story."

Public journalism enters the dialogue here. Journalists, it says, would do well to assume that their own fortunes depend on the fate of America's civic culture. The way to secure a vital future for the press is to strengthen, in any practical way that can be found, all the forces that pull people into civic affairs, engage them in the give-and-take of political dialogue, make participants out of spectators, and illuminate the promise of public life. The press itself can be one of those forces, and a deeper professional identity can be fashioned around these central themes.

As most of them realize, journalists do more than furnish us with facts. They frame and narrate the story of our common life. This story needs to provoke and challenge as much as it informs and entertains. In every community and about the nation as a whole, there are disturbing and depressing tales to be told. If the press does not commit to telling them, well and often, its demise will be deserved. But there are ways of facing even the darkest facts that leave us open to the task of remaking them. As storytellers journalists find their deepest challenge here. Without relinquishing their stance as observers and critics, they can try to nourish a particular understanding of American society: not an audience of savvy spectators nor a class of information-rich consumers, but a nation of citizens with common problems, an inventive spirit, and a rich participatory tradition.

Some may consider the ideal of engaged citizenship unreachable or nostalgic, but others are already finding within it a renewed sense of purpose and a boost to flagging spirits. As they experiment with public journalism, they are struggling to learn a great lesson, namely, that *Democracy in America*, the title of Alexis de Tocqueville's famous work, is the implied subtitle for every serious story a journalist writes. Reaching this insight involves a long process of self-inquiry, and making good on its promise requires institutional change. But this is a test many other professions will face as they learn to cope with public mistrust and changing expectations.[13]

The American press is no creature of the state, but it is a kind of political institution and has a legitimate stake in whether politics works for all or becomes the professional playground of a privileged few. Journalists should be allowed to demonstrate they care whether America's civic traditions hold their own or dissolve away amid the attractions of a consumer culture. To the spreading cynicism that has become such an occupational hazard in journalism, a potent corrective is required—some clear and compelling alternatives to the familiar metaphors of politics-as-sports and public-life-as-battlefield.

What permits public life to go well, what encourages people to find common interests and common work, what brings forth our latent desire to understand each other—another kind of "politics" needs to be heard and seen, alongside the familiar tales of money, power and manipulation. Public journalism is not about "good news" or cheering people up. But it does contend that the press, without straining to report an illusory consensus or wishing away conflict and strife, can be far more assertive in promoting the kind of public dialogue that might get us somewhere, whether the "us" is a neighborhood beset by street crime, a city fighting to secure its economic base, or a nation debating affirmative action. "When politics goes well," writes the philosopher Michael Sandel, "we can know a good in common that we cannot know alone."[14] The press can try to make public life "go well" in Sandel's sense, and hope for a restoration of its authority, some relief from the grim spiral of cynicism and mistrust.

Finally, journalism can do all this without departing from its central mission to inform and enlighten, without surrendering its important role as watchdog and critic, without boring us with civics lessons or hyping itself as the answer to all our ills. The task is broad and difficult, but there is enough talent and dedication in the American press to claim a far more constructive role in public life. Many journalists wish to do just that, and leaders in the profession need to ask themselves how they can mobilize that lingering commitment.

Our national adventure is taking a wide and dangerous turn. We are entering an age when problems are deep-set and government cannot necessarily provide the answer, when citizens need to claim a place at the table or watch the table get spirited away, when democracy will either become a willed achievement or a sentimental dream. Journalists should not huddle together in the press box, wondering how the story will come out. They need to rejoin the American experiment. But first they will have to drop the devastating illusion of themselves as bystanders, "watching the idiots screw it up." Public journalism begins there.

1/CHALLENGING THE CULTURE OF THE PRESS

"We are going to be loathed and despised for one reason or another no matter what we do. That's the goal; that's our job. . . ." These are the words of Lesley Stahl, the longtime Washington correspondent for CBS News and former host of "Face the Nation."[1] Stahl speaks for many of her colleagues when she views hostility toward the press as proof of a job well done.

The rest of us may be more struck by the sadness of Stahl's attitude. Any profession that has to feel "loathed and despised" in order to accomplish its goals has either the wrong goals or an inhuman burden to bear. According to a 1994 study by the Times Mirror Company, 71 percent of Americans say the press now "gets in the way of society solving its problems."[2] This might be seen, by Stahl and others of like mind, as evidence of a sound performance. More likely, it is a sign of something awry in the journalist's universe, a confusion of priorities that has not gone undetected by the wider public.

Now listen to Teresa Hanafin, city editor of the *Boston Globe*, reflecting on her job description at a seminar on public journalism:

> I have increasingly seen my role as a journalist as finding common ground. I am extremely offended by the Crossfire mentality that exists in political life. . . . It is extremely unproductive; it is even destructive at times. It consists of angry sound bites that mean nothing and serve no purpose but to polarize. . . .
>
> So I have moved from the detached, objective person— just spewing out reams of information and hoping on good faith that people will take the information and act—

7

to realizing that we have to be more of a player in helping
people act on that information. And that very often does
mean searching out the middle ground, some kind of place
where they can come together.[3]

Around the country, there are journalists wrestling with the problems that concern Hanafin: the deterioration of public dialogue, the
reduction of politics to a sporting match, the emptiness and cynicism
that so characterize our public life, and the complicity of the press in
all these trends. In places like Wichita, Norfolk, Charlotte, and
Madison, enterprising journalists are returning to first principles in
an effort to assess what has gone wrong with their profession.

A surprising discovery often comes their way: those first principles
are not canons of journalism but conditions of political life. A public
that is engaged as well as informed, a polity that can deliberate as well
as debate, communities that not only know about but can also act
upon their problems, readers who think of themselves as citizens as
well as consumers of the news—these are necessary conditions for a
responsible and effective press. "Public journalism" and "civic journalism" are names the reformers give to the approach they are beginning to devise.

One of the striking things about the culture of the American press,
which exerts such a strong influence on its members, is how conservative it is—conservative about journalism.[4] There are a variety of reasons for this. Consider first the pressures that bear on the people who
produce the news: the conflicting demands of audiences, media owners, political figures, sources, and especially the daily pressure of dead-
lines, a "monster" that has to be fed, whether the food is ready or not.
Add to these the comparatively thin credentials of the journalist as a
maker of professional judgments: no advanced training or licensing,
no white lab coat, no obscure vocabulary to intimidate the layperson,
no particular expertise in most of the subjects explored in the news, no
scientific method or formal peer review. As press scholar Michael
Schudson puts it, "Journalism is an uninsulated profession."[5]

One result is that journalists are highly vulnerable to criticism
that their decisions are arbitrary or unfair. Indeed, if there is one
proposition that unites Americans across the political and cultural
spectrum, it may be that the news media are "biased"—although the
charge means different things to different groups and is often highly
politicized. Add to the complaints about bias the enormous power the
press still has, for good or ill, and it becomes easier to understand the
conservative impulse—sticking with routines and sticking together.

Journalists do as their peers do, they do as they have always done, in part because they lack the cultural protections and instant authority afforded doctors by their medical expertise, professors by their PhDs, political leaders by their victories at the polls. "All we own is our credibility" is a typical refrain, and this perception of weakness breeds an understandable suspicion of ringing calls for change.

Beyond "credibility," however, is another claim to ownership the press routinely mounts: its claim on the First Amendment. Although the Constitution refers to state censors, not civilian critics, the journalist's reading of the First Amendment (hands off the press) is often extended to every sort of threatening voice, giving the culture an additional fortification against outside influence.[6] Martin Linsky, who has experience as a journalist, scholar, and public official, notes that "the press is a substantial barrier to overcome" for those "attempting to move toward a richer, more participatory . . . dialogue on public affairs." People in journalism "want to believe that the nature and quality of dialogue about public issues is none of their business, that they just report the news," he writes.[7] Michael Janeway, former editor of the *Boston Globe* and now a journalism dean at Northwestern University, elaborates:

> The press says as a matter of professional identity, and I myself have said as a journalist, that our business is facts, the public has a right to know them, freedom has a price, we let the chips fall where they may, we are not in the philosophy business. . . . It says, no one got into this business to be loved, weighty reflection about our role is for journalism schools and op-ed pages, not for the reporter and the editor under the gun or on the trail of the next Watergate.[8]

What results from these attitudes is an odd combination of total exposure—the news is open to criticism from every quarter every day—and professional insularity, as journalists turn to each other for clues as to how to behave, what to value, which stories to chase. When this pattern leaves them feeling out of touch with "real people," as it inevitably does, the temptation is to veer in the opposite direction—toward sensational items that promise to lure in a reluctant audience even as they corrode the journalist's self-respect and erase the distinction between "journalism" and the "media." Howard Kurtz of the *Washington Post,* who reports on the press, has taken note of these contradictory tendencies in his book *Media Circus.* He writes of "a fatal disconnection, a growing gap between editors and

reporters on the one hand and consumers of news on the other."
Kurtz continues:

> My incestuous profession has become increasingly self-
> absorbed, even as its practitioners wring their hands about why
> fewer people seem to be listening. I hear this depressing talk
> every day, in newsroom meetings, in causal conversations, in
> my colleagues' bitter jokes about toiling for a dying business. .
> . . Yet we in this business have gone a long way toward squan-
> dering our natural advantages. For too long we have published
> newspapers aimed at other journalists—talking to ourselves,
> really, and to the insiders we gossip with—and paying scant
> attention to our readers. . . . Where once newspapers were at
> the very heart of the national conversation, they now seem
> remote, arrogant, part of the governing elite. Where once news-
> papers embodied cultural values, they now seem mired in a
> tabloid culture that gorges itself on sex and sleaze.[9]

An "incestuous profession" that is warned so bluntly by one of its
leading members would seem to be in need of significant change—
something that could jog complacent minds, enlist creative energies,
and strike a mood of urgency among those seeking a better way. But
"seeking a better way" hardly gets the juices flowing in most newsrooms, where "print truth and raise hell" describes the favored ethic.
"If your mother says she loves you, check it out," a favorite newsroom
crack, captures the self-image of the journalist as an unrelenting skep-
tic. Trained in the arts of suspicion, accustomed to demanding that
others respond to their questions, journalists make poor targets for
inspirational rhetoric, for any call to check their values and change
their ways.

All of which makes the initial gropings of the public journalists
so interesting to contemplate. They are far from having the answer to
all that ails the press. They have not discovered any magic formula.
What "success" means in their evolving approach is not well understood. Indeed, public journalism is at times an elusive thing, more of
an inclination than a set of techniques or a clear code of conduct. This
is frustrating to critics who want to get a handle on the phenomenon;
but it is also a clue to the phenomenon itself.

These are the thoughts of Davis Merritt, editor of the *Wichita
Eagle*, and the most visible proponent of public journalism within the
press:

Simply "telling the news" of a complex society does little to help solve basic problems, for we have spent years detailing them, analyzing them, and raising alarms about them, but still they persist.

Yet many journalists reject the suggestion that there is, or could be, a broader journalistic role than the one we have played. The public, their philosophy declares, must simply take the divinely defined and delivered news and do the best it can. Journalists, they contend, must maintain a pristine distance, a contrived indifference to outcomes, else the news product be contaminated. . . .

So pinched a view ignores a practical reality: Our profession's very existence depends on the viability of public life. A public that does not attend to public affairs, that retreats deeply into private life and concerns, has no need of journalists and journalism.[10]

While some in the press, as Kurtz noted, "wring their hands about why fewer people seem to be listening," journalists like Merritt are listening to more people outside of journalism, searching for a stronger connection between themselves and ordinary citizens, taking more responsibility for the quality of public discussion, and wondering if they can't do more to help make democracy work.

2/DEBATING PUBLIC JOURNALISM

So far there has been a fair amount of criticism and resistance toward public journalism from journalists who have heard or read about the approach.[1] It has been charged with being: 1) no real departure from what has always been done by good journalists in good newsrooms; 2) a misguided if well-intentioned effort that mistakes journalism for community organizing or a social service agency; 3) a dangerous intrusion of "advocacy" into the politically neutral space of the news; 4) a marketing gimmick or public relations stunt that substitutes a feel-good populism for the investment in news gathering that serious journalism demands; 5) a surrender of professional judgment to the whims of the mass audience.

In a column on civic journalism, Max Frankel, former executive editor of the *New York Times*, added a further criticism: "American journalism sorely needs improvement," Frankel wrote. "But redefining journalism as a quest for a better tomorrow will never compensate for its poor performance at explaining yesterday. Reporters, editors and publishers have their hands full learning to tell it right. They should leave reforms to the reformers."[2] Richard Harwood, former ombudsman of the *Washington Post*, agrees: "The press already has credibility problems, based on the public perception that it is an arrogant, self-serving institution that more aggravates than cures the social illnesses that afflict us. To anoint ourselves now as leaders of a new American reformation may be a little more than the market will bear."[3] For Maxwell King, editor of the *Philadelphia Inquirer*, public journalism tinkers recklessly with the independence of the press. "The traditional rules about the distance and impartiality of reporters from their subjects are a key source of our strength," King said. "It is crazy to break those rules, and there is no reason to break those rules."[4]

The editors and reporters who have been experimenting with public journalism share many of these concerns. They worry about becoming "too involved" in a process that rightfully belongs to the citizenry. They wish to retain their independence, of course, and they are aware of the subtle forms that compromise can take. But they also recognize something the critics tend to overlook: "detachment" and "independence" have their ignoble sides, as when journalists come to see themselves as spectators "watching the idiots screw it up" or as handicappers, chatting about the outcome of a game they obviously disdain.

Public journalism must negotiate between the dangers of excess involvement on the one hand and excess indifference on the other. This is a difficult test of professional judgment, for it means entering a territory where there are no clear rules, only broad goals: creating discussion, furthering participation, aiding in public problem-solving, re-connecting citizens to public life. Far from compromising professional standards, the serious pursuit of these aims may help restore public confidence in the press. Rather than engage on this point, where there is plenty to debate, critics tend to repeat the "advocacy" charge, which is little more than a straw man.

As I will later show, some of the more daring experiments do place journalists in a catalytic or convening role. But there is a clear difference between bringing people to the table and telling them what to decide, between creating discussion and dominating it, between helping citizens get involved and doing their work for them. I have sometimes used the phrase "proactive neutrality" to describe the public journalist's approach. It is neutral because it prescribes no chosen solution and favors no particular party of interest. It is proactive in its belief that journalism can in certain cases intervene in the service of broad public values without compromising its integrity.

A word like "intervene" raises eyebrows, naturally. But it is important to establish that the press is already interventionist in dozens of ways that have become standard practice, from investigative reporting to political handicapping. The notion that journalists simply "tell it like it is" (Max Frankel's words), that they observe the scene without exerting any influence upon it, is impossible to square with their daily experience—to say nothing of those in politics and civic life, who must factor in the peculiarities of press behavior at every turn.[5]

This is not to say that reporting is inevitably biased; nor is it intended to mock the struggle for a disinterested truth. The press does in fact figure prominently in what happens in the public world, and in who or what gets noticed or fades from view. Serious journalists actually seek this kind of influence; they are proud when their reporting both tells the truth and "sets the agenda." Nothing pleases them more than forcing government to respond to what they report.

It is remarkable how quickly such facts disappear in the sometimes heated debate over public journalism. What ought to be discussed is not whether the press should be "involved" or "detached,"
but the best kind of involvement, the nature of the press's legitimate
influence, the values that lie beneath its own agenda. There is considerable room for debate on these issues, and those experimenting with
public journalism welcome the exchange. Not, however, if they have to
establish what should be an acknowledged fact: journalism is no daily
mirror of events but a story with themes chosen by journalists.

Those who know how the political game works know that the
press is deeply involved. If journalists must choose between their hard-
won knowledge of political reality and the professional fiction of an
"uninvolved" press, they will usually take reality. Consider the foam-
ing indictment of Washington political culture written by former *New
York Times* reporter Michael Kelly in the paper's Sunday magazine.
Throughout Washington, Kelly wrote, "image" had overtaken any genuine concern for substance. Fully implicated in this debasement of
politics was the national press corps, which was promoting a certain
way of seeing the world. "Obsessed with the appearance of things,"
journalists make themselves "susceptible to the machinations of the
image-makers." The press "has become as faddish as a teenager, vac-
illating in its attitudes towards the powers that be, going from bubbling enthusiasm to hysterical anger, from cheering all that the
President says to denouncing all that the President does."

The "press pack," as Kelly called it, "rewards, with glowing praise,
triumphs of form over content, medium well-turned phrases, smart
photo ops, effective P.R. stunts. But it is also unhappily aware of its
own vulnerability, and exacts a perverse revenge by seizing on the
slightest misstep, the smallest deviation from the perfect image. . . ."
Honorable enough to include himself, Kelly offered some examples
of his own dispatches for the *Times,* little "bits of fatuousness" he wrote
that tried to "fashion reality out of perceptions" and thus keep the
game of images going.[6]

Observations like these—in which the press helps create the current political climate—have become standard fare among journalists, who are forced by their own ethic of honesty to see the press as an
actor on the public stage. Like Kelly, civic journalism rejects the illusion of the journalist as a bystander. But it goes on from there to try to
reconcile this reality with the democratic ideals at the heart of the
American press. Public journalism seeks a stronger civic base from
which the press can operate in framing the news and employing its
influence. Rather than elevate image over reality (as Kelly says his

colleagues have), why not elevate "participatory democracy" and "deliberative dialogue" over "media manipulation?" Asking such questions has nothing to do with "anointing" journalism as lead force in an "American reformation." The point is to engage citizens and communities in the work of solving problems, not for journalists to take over the process. Frankel and Harwood fail to grasp this, but they are hardly alone. Harry Rosenfeld, editor of the Albany *Times-Union*, objects to civic journalism because it "seeks to dedicate the resources of the craft to help implement solutions, including the personal participation of staffers in formulating remedies that the newspaper will then write about and promote."[7] Rosenfeld cites no examples and quotes no one associated with public journalism. Nor could he, for his description is a fantasy, calculated to provoke every journalist's worst fears.

William Woo, editor of the St. Louis *Post-Dispatch*, asks in a speech critical of public journalism whether a newspaper can "objectively report on a burning community issue when the editor sits on the commission that is promoting a particular point of view on the matter."[8] Woo would be hard-pressed to find any such editors, at least any with visible ties to public journalism. His example is almost entirely without factual basis. But this is the kind of thing that is repeatedly said in a "debate" that rarely rises to the issue at hand: What should journalists do about the various ills that afflict public life and the growing disconnect between themselves and the public? Should they pretend that they're not "involved?" Or, recognizing the dangers of doing too much, should they do what they can to improve public life and repair the breach between citizens and the press?

Public journalism does not apologize for having an agenda, which includes things like a more engaged and deliberative public, a more workable civic climate, a better political debate. Even broad values like these are too much, however, for one of the movement's most prominent critics, Leonard Downie, executive editor of the *Washington Post*. Downie objects to public journalists "deciding what good citizenship is and force-feeding it to citizens and candidates" by "encouraging citizens to vote" or pressuring "candidates to participate in a dialogue with voters." Public journalism is a bad idea, he says, because it makes journalists into "actors on the political stage."[9]

Downie at least mentions things that resemble what civic journalists believe: citizens should vote, candidates should engage us in dialogue. His contention that journalists have no business "deciding what good citizenship is" is provocative because it illustrates the limits of neutrality in the press. Should journalists really avoid coming to *any* conclusions about what "good citizenship" involves or requires?

Downie seems to say so, and yet from reading the *Washington Post*, anyone can detect the following convictions at work: A good citizen is an informed citizen. Good citizens get both sides of the story and decide for themselves. Good citizens follow foreign affairs. Good citizens like a range of opinion to sample in the morning.

Shall we denounce Downie for "force feeding" these beliefs to innocent readers of the *Post*? We could, but that would be rather uncivil. What we ought to be discussing, after all, are competing views of citizenship and how they may lead to different forms of journalism. Downie has his theory of what a good citizen is *and bases his journalism upon it*. Public journalism may have a different view. Let the best view win!

But this is exactly where the debate has not gone because too many in the press prefer to claim that they have no view of citizenship, no image of political life embedded in their routines, no particular understanding of democracy to question and perhaps revise in the face of the widening disconnect. Public journalism steers clear of this abuse of neutrality. It argues openly for citizens as participants, politics as problem solving, democracy as thoughtful deliberation. These, it says, are sound beliefs on which to base a revitalized press. They have a neutral core to them, but they are values nonetheless—choices journalists might make—and they can be defended as intelligent choices.

Public journalists further believe in listening more carefully to citizens' concerns, starting the engines of journalism closer to the point where citizens begin.[10] In this they seek to understand some of the reasons why Americans increasingly hate politics and disdain serious journalism. Listening well to a wider range of people is thus the civic journalist's first commandment. But to equate this approach with a "marketing" ethic is inaccurate and unfair. It suggests no difference between listening to citizens and pandering to readers. And it fails to account for the experience of journalists who have found "listening well" a demanding and satisfying professional challenge.

Starting where citizens start does not mean ending where citizens end; nor does it mean recycling readers' desires and diluting the serious content of the news. Properly approached, public journalism is about challenging people to interact with journalists and with each other as concerned citizens rather than as victims, consumers, or bystanders.

Are all these things what good journalism already does? Not according to those who did it one way, and are now trying it another. Here is Cole Campbell, editor of the *Virginian-Pilot* in Norfolk, giving his view of what public journalism involves:

We [at the Pilot] have learned that, to improve our work and revitalize our craft, we must live in two worlds—the world of ideas and the world of action. We have begun to peel back the layers of our unexamined newsroom ideology to learn what frames our view of public life. We are coming to realize that deliberative democracy may hold more possibilities than representative democracy, and that covering democracy one way can be just as legitimate as covering it another. We have gone immediately into the field reporting and writing our stories in new ways, not as special projects but as daily field tests. And we have begun to build a deliberative newsroom, where journalists are taking charge of their shared professional destiny.

We have learned that it is all right to respect the people of [the Norfolk area] as consumers, who need or prefer certain features of our newspaper, and as citizens, who see public life in a far more encompassing way than we journalists do. And we have learned to respect citizens as partners in a continuing conversation about abortion, water supplies, neighborhood zoning, the Voting Rights Act, school prayer, political character and even the praying away of hurricanes by our neighbor, Pat Robertson.

. . . We are learning to hold citizens accountable, not only by asking them to reconcile their beliefs with contradictory evidence but also by asking them to spell out their own responsibility for the health of their community.

. . . We are holding public figures and institutions more accountable to the concerns of the citizens they serve by making explicit in our coverage what those concerns are.[11]

The civic approach is frequently called "just good journalism" by those impatient with the rhetoric of novelty that sometimes suffuses the idea. But no one in public journalism cares whether the approach is considered old or new. They simply say it is needed.

3/AMERICAN JOURNALISM IS IN TROUBLE

To understand why the debate over public journalism matters, it is helpful to begin with a wider view of the predicament facing journalists in the United States. Under the heading of "journalist" belong all those, in any medium, who report and comment on the contemporary scene with some intention of making sense of it. "Journalism" is what these people do. But it is also how they explain and justify what they do, and how the rest of us understand it. Our expectations for journalism are part of what the thing is.

"The press" denotes journalism as an institution, but it is important not to equate this with something else now called "the media." While the media's future seems bright, if highly unpredictable, the press is in considerably more trouble. Unless we learn to separate the fortunes of the two, journalism as a public art will never get the defense it deserves. The efforts of the public journalists should be seen in the proper context: they are struggling to place journalism within a public frame—where what becomes of democracy, civic life, and politics in America will determine what happens to the press.

The story I will tell might be called "six crises for the American press." But since the word "crisis" is overworked, I will refer instead to six alarm bells (economic, technological, political, occupational, spiritual, intellectual) that are ringing for journalists at present. Most of them have been heard and discussed by thoughtful people in the field, along with some of their academic counterparts. But there is no consensus on what ought to be done, or indeed on what journalists can do as employees of profit-making companies on the one hand, and professionals with a public identity on the other.

SIX ALARM BELLS FOR THE AMERICAN PRESS

1. The Economic Alarm

The problem of the deteriorating economic base for journalism is usually understood as one of disappearing audiences, with special attention paid to the long-term decline in newspaper readership.[1] To take one measure of this decline, in a March 1995 national survey, only 45 percent of Americans said they had read a daily newspaper the previous day, down from 58 percent in February 1994 and from 71 percent in a comparable study in 1965.[2] Some of the measures taken to combat this threat seem to journalists worse than the threat itself, particularly the rise of a "marketing" ethic in which the pursuit of lost readers overtakes the search for news, erodes professional judgment, and eviscerates a proud tradition of public service.[3]

In a provocative 1990 essay, Philip Meyer, a journalism scholar at the University of North Carolina, offered another view of the problem.[4] It is not only that readers are disappearing (they are) or that advertisers have alternatives available to them (they do). Rather, the underlying economic rationale for journalism needs to be rethought. In the past, Meyer reminds us, the independence of journalism from the business operation was not a gift from high-minded owners; it was a smart strategy for the newspaper as a business. What advertisers purchased was the credibility of the paper, and to produce this credibility was the job of the newsroom. The logical way was to grant independence to the editorial voice.

Thus grew the church-state separation as a familiar characteristic of the better newsrooms, with journalists insulated from the demands of the advertising and circulation departments. Thus developed the professional ethic of objectivity, distance, and detachment. With it came what Meyer calls "the characteristic moral profile" of the American journalist: a "lone hero wandering from market to market like the archetypal cowboy of the movies, settling scores on behalf of the common man against the rich and the powerful."[5] All of these things have their own rationale within journalism. But Meyer is interested in their economic logic; what made a particular form of journalism compatible with a specific commercial enterprise. So he posits that if advertisers have other ways of delivering their messages, then journalists may have to create something that has even more value than the credibility they once lent to the newspaper.

Similarly, if people are awash in information, then journalists may need to offer something that has even more value than additional items dumped into the daily data stream. Here, then, is the heart of the

economic challenge facing journalism. It is not only the disappear-
ance of readers, or the reluctance of advertisers, or the presence of the
dreaded MBAs in the sacred space of the newsroom. It is a profound
uncertainty about what it is that journalists produce in the first place.
In the language of economics, what value have journalists added, and
how can they convert this into a reasonably secure economic base?

The falloff in newspaper readership is indeed disturbing, especially when the appallingly low rates for young people are highlighted.[6]
But capturing more readers, viewers, and listeners is not the only issue,
for unless the lure is a journalism worth doing, the recaptured audience lends the journalist no real support. Harold Evans, former editor
of the London *Times*, put it well when he said that the challenge "is
not to stay in business—it is to stay in journalism."[7] No one yet knows
how to meet this challenge.

2. The Technology Alarm

This is related to the economic crisis but goes well beyond it. A new
communication network is emerging, but no one knows what place
it will give to serious journalism. "In newsrooms across the country,
we're scared," said Maxwell King of the *Philadelphia Inquirer* in 1993.
"We're worried . . . [that] when the technological wonders of the next
couple decades are upon us, there won't be much left of our end of
the business."[8]

King's concerns are well-founded. As more and more data
become available, as delivery systems multiply and the mass audience
fragments, it becomes harder and harder to see what a journalist's role
is. Information is no longer scarce. Direct links that remove the filter
between source and audience are more and more prevalent. Consumer choice seems to be on the rise. A "one-to-many" communication pattern—typical of newspapers and television—is being slowly
replaced by a "many-to-many" system more akin to the telephone
system, a web of connections where data flows freely. In cyberspace,
how do we understand the figure of the journalist, as a person doing
what sort of things? It is possible to imagine new forms of journalism
emerging, but no one knows yet how to find them or fund them.

The technology alarm has caught the attention of some of the most
experienced minds in the press.[9] In 1994 and 1995, the Nieman
Foundation at Harvard University, led by its farsighted curator, Bill
Kovach, organized high-level conferences on how to preserve "public
interest journalism" in the emerging era of on-line communication. In
convening the first conference, Kovach recognized that the "system in
which journalism is embedded" is due for a major transformation as

media companies rush to exploit the commercial potential of new technologies. The forces at work in this new information environment will undoubtedly shape the future of journalism. But as Kovach observed, "they do not take as their primary obligation the further-ance of journalism in the public interest."[10] Unless journalists and their defenders become familiar with the technology "and active in shaping the decisions that will be made about its uses," then "other forces with more powerful interests will make those decisions."

Meeting this challenge is made more difficult by the dual identi-ties of most journalists. On the one hand they are employees of media companies that own huge stakes in the coming transformation. On the other hand, they are members of a profession—or as some prefer, a craft—that matters because it stands for something more than the next business opportunity. For journalists as employees the technol-ogy challenge is distinct from professional concerns: How can my company adapt to the new information environment and produce something (whether "journalism" or not) that people will pay for? Thus, technology differentiates the prospects for the press from those of the business of communications—the media. And as Kovach noted after the second Nieman conference, "Today it seems anyone and everyone, from the phone company to a computer hacker in Oslo, is in the business of making news available."[11]

3. The Political Alarm

This bell went off loudly after the dispiriting 1988 campaign, but the underlying problem is deeper than 1988 revealed—and far deeper than trends in voter turnout. Politics is not working well, and the press seems caught up in this failure.

For years journalists and academic observers have worried aloud about the fallout from certain predictable patterns in the press treat-ment of politics: the "feeding frenzies," in which public figures become the target of an overzealous press pack; the "horse race" angle that treats politics as little more than a sporting match; the obsession with political strategy and the "who's up, who's down" game of savvy insid-ers; the insufficient attention paid to serious issues of public policy as journalists compete with each other and with a tabloid culture that shows less and less restraint. These traps are well documented.[12] The way out of them has yet to be shown.

The rise of the so-called new media has contributed to the breach between the traditional press and the public.[13] Such developments as "Larry King Live," MTV, C-SPAN, talk radio, on-line chat rooms, and the televised "town meeting" may have little in common. But one thing they share is their advantage over traditional journalism in creating a livable space for political talk, one that does not instantly repel people with the sense that political dialogue has nothing to offer. "Address our needs, not your needs" was perhaps the most memorable line from the most memorable event of 1992—the second presidential debate in Richmond. It was spoken by a citizen to the candidates, but it might have easily been said to the press.

Although many journalists hesitate to think it, the press is itself a political institution. Like all institutions, it ultimately depends on public support, and its support has been dwindling. Consider the startling figures developed by Yankelovich Partners, who ask the same questions year after year in order to provide reliable benchmarks. In 1988, 55 percent of Americans said they had "a great deal of confidence" in news reports on television. By 1993, that number was down to 25 percent. In 1988, 50 percent said they had "a great deal of confidence" in news from newspapers; by 1993 the figure had dropped to 20 percent. For magazines, the drop was from 38 to 12 percent.[14] Something is happening here. While all public institutions have suffered a decline in public trust, the drop in popular confidence in the press has been swift and dramatic in recent years.

Many journalists pride themselves on their mature, unblinkered view of the political scene, often with good reason. But the political maturity of the press as an institution is another matter. That will come only when journalists are able to view themselves as political actors of a sort—with some responsibility for what happens in politics, with some stake in the health of the political system, and with some need for public support. They are not at that point yet, and that is confounding any efforts to address the political alarm bell.

4. The Occupational Alarm

According to a 1992 study of 1,410 journalists in the United States, one in five expect to leave the field within a few years, double the figure from a decade earlier. Other findings confirm a growing sense of disaffection in newsrooms. In 1971, 49 percent of those surveyed said they were very satisfied with their jobs. In 1983, some 40 percent still reported high satisfaction. By 1992, that figure was down to 27 percent.[15] It is not much fun to come to work, more and more journalists report. Newsrooms are becoming hostile places as new demands put stress on old routines.[16]

In a 1995 cover story called "The Thrill Is Gone," *American Journalism Review* observed, "Angst and anxiety are pandemic across American newsrooms, as newspaper people collectively sense the end of an era."

A 1992 pamphlet from the Poynter Institute for Media Studies, entitled *Call for Leadership*, conveyed this anxious mood in the press. Addressed to "all who treasure the news business," at "a time of trouble for American journalism and the public it serves," the document read. Reporters are suspicious of the motives of their editors. The editors worry about the values of business managers. Some news organizations are in turmoil, fighting what amounts to a cultural cold war over values and resources."[17]

A related problem involves what many see as a decline in professional standards. Feeling pressure from the tabloid media, journalists have slid into practices they once would have shunned as a violation of their code.[18] The clearest example is reporting rumors about the private lives of public figures, which one scholar calls "the single most disturbing development in modern journalism."[19] Jack Nelson, Washington bureau chief for the *Los Angeles Times*, sees other worrisome trends:

> We've lowered our standards on what we put in the paper these days. . . . We publish stories that are based on a single source or a questionable source. We raise questions we don't answer. We jump to conclusions without having solid evidence. . . . We let the tabloids dictate the pace. We run stories based on relatively little solid evidence and figure if we call up the person to ask for his reaction, we're covered.[20]

While many are alarmed by such developments, others see an ethical free-for-all as virtually unavoidable. As Weston Kosova, now a reporter for *Newsweek*, puts it, "Ethics imply professional standards. But journalism isn't a profession, it's a trade." In his view, "there is no common standard of professional behavior that all journalists adhere to on pain of banishment from the ranks."[21]

Of course journalists cannot be "banished" the way lawyers can be disbarred. But those who claim professional prerogatives cannot easily disclaim the need for common and defensible standards. When the press says to us, "We'll ask the questions of your elected officials, we'll examine the character of candidates to high office, we'll determine what's important for you to know," it is asking to be seen as a profession, with a custodial duty to the public it serves. On the whole, ethical standards have climbed dramatically in journalism in the course of this century; the press is now more educated and better trained than at any time in its history. But this only makes the recent slippage in conduct more worrisome—journalists know better and once aspired to better. Tom Rosenstiel, former media reporter for the *Los Angeles Times*, points out that the press can distinguish itself from the tabloid culture only by demonstrating that it is "engaged in public service and is committed to high standards of accuracy and proof."[22]

The occupational alarm points to the interior culture of the press. Can it meet the challenge of "staying in journalism," while at the same time becoming more diverse, more democratic, more imaginative—and even more human? Can it recover a sense of professional duty and address the problem of declining standards despite the current mood of anxiety and mistrust? There are many signs of strain showing.

5. The Spiritual Alarm

Many of the occupational troubles are related to economic pressures and management changes. However, some of them emerge from an even deeper source—the lack of any affirmative vision, something inspiring that journalists can work toward or believe in. By a "spiritual" alarm I mean an empty answer to the question: What are we doing all this for? What we are we trying to achieve here? Where are our deepest sources of inspiration? How can we tap them to move forward against difficult odds?

In my experience, journalists talk easily about what they're "against." They're on guard against any threat to the First Amendment. As "watchdogs," they protect against misdeeds in government. They labor against the truth-shading tactics of politicians and spin doctors. They are naturally against anyone coming into the newsroom to tell them what to do. But occasionally it is necessary to ask: What are journalists *for*? To put a slight stronger edge on it, what do they stand for?

Often the answer seems to be a snarling and relentless cynicism—a categorical mistrust of all public figures. If the American press has a belief system, it tends toward the cultivation of a generalized disbelief. The journalist's characteristic way of seeing is to see through the phony facade, the arranged impression. If there's an identifiable tone, it is that of the zealous prosecutor, in search of the hidden motive or the telling lie.[23] Here the professional culture of the press is powerfully at work. What reporters are likely to fear is not the corrosion of their souls, but the judgment of their colleagues that they have been "naïve."

The dynamic is most visible in Washington journalism. Ruth Marcus, a reporter for the *Washington Post*, describes her own experience with the White House press corps:

> It is like junior high school. I have never met a group of people who complain more about what they are doing. It's an

ethos of disgruntlement—of which cynicism is a part. And in the group ethos, naiveté is the hugest sin of all. Nothing could make you look more stupid than saying, "I think, gee, they're doing this because they're right." There's almost a bidding war of cynicism.[24]

Those impatient with the charge of excessive cynicism often reply by emphasizing the burden of their experience—the daily ritual of being manipulated or lied to, the disillusionment following the Vietnam era and Watergate, the far greater cynicism on display in government and business, the public's appetite for sensational stories and negative campaigns.[25] Framed this way, the conflict appears to pit the realist's mournful insistence on a hard-won truth (governments lie, officials evade, people respond to the negative) against the fuzzy idealism of the "naïve" observer, wistfully hoping for more civility and virtue in public life.

There is much that escapes such a crude contrast, including any ecological understanding of the press and political actors. Consider the self-sustaining cycle described by Paul Taylor, a former political reporter for the *Washington Post*. "We are carriers, as well as chroniclers of the prevailing disenchantment with public life," he wrote. "The more cynical the news reporters and news consumers have become, the more image-manipulating, demagogic and risk-averse the newsmakers have become. And so our cynicism begets their fakery, and their fakery our cynicism, and so on."[26]

From Taylor's perspective, the journalist's experience is inseparable from the journalist's behavior: cynical assumptions, carried along by the press, help produce cynical responses as a poisonous climate overtakes the political scene. Journalists may say they're just reporting on such a climate, but in their hearts they know they are also producing it. As Katharine Q. Seelye of the *New York Times* observed in passing, "Modern American culture is loud and adversarial, and politics reflects the culture. And the ever-adversarial, conflict-seeking press helps shape the politics."[27]

If the press "helps shape the politics" we have now, then presumably it can shape the politics we need. In fact, it may have to do so simply to survive. For beneath the hardened "realism" of the cynical reporter lies a whopping illusion: that publics eager to see the veil stripped from politics will magically reappear each day to provide the journalist with an attentive audience. The more likely result is that people will ignore the news as they come to conclude that no honest leaders exist, no genuine debate can be had, no one cares much whether problems are solved, and therefore politics and journalism are a waste of time. According to Howard Kurtz this reaction has already set in. "The plain fact," he wrote recently, "is that much of the American public has simply tuned out the news—that is, the kind of traditional news, heavily laden with politicians and official proceedings, routinely covered by the mainstream press. These people see journalists as messengers from another world."[28]

Aligning the world of the experienced journalist with a world the rest of us can share, while at the same time demanding that truth be told, is an exceedingly difficult task. It means asking: What values can discipline the journalist's skepticism to prevent it from lapsing into a cynical, jeering stance? What sort of people do journalists truly wish to be, and how can they prevent the rhythms of their experience from undermining that larger quest? Just as politicians can appeal to the best or the worst in us—and prove "accurate" in both directions—so can journalism either lift us up or drag us down, depending on what kind of "accuracy" it aims for. Finding a truth that does not eviscerate hope is thus the heart of the journalist's spiritual challenge.

6. The Intellectual Alarm

As many of the preceding quotations illustrate, thoughtful people in the press worry about the economic, technological, political, occupational and spiritual warning signs. Less often do they acknowledge an intellectual problem in journalism that is growing more and more severe. The key concepts journalists employ to explain themselves and their craft don't work very well. They offer little help in navigating the future; they even fail to describe the present.

Take the commonsense notion that "information" is what the press provides. This is not a conceptually rich description of the skills and talents that distinguish "journalism" from any other information service. It says nothing about the forms of judgment that are essential to sound journalism, the ways in which a news organization *reduces* rather than "produces" information, the delicate task of framing the news that reporters and editors routinely perform.

Aware of the information glut, journalists will sometimes observe that they need to go beyond a simple presentation of news to offer additional depth. Words like "context," "interpretation," and "analysis" enter the discussion. These things are works of mind, not naturally occurring phenomena: context cannot be located in the events to be contextualized; interpretations do not spring from the facts themselves; analysis won't come from the analyzed. They are only as good as the "software"—the ideas about society and economy, power and politics, human nature and contemporary culture—from which they arise.

The problem is not that journalists lack such ideas; rather, they lack a language for describing and improving them, for making their vision more explicit in order to apply a sharpened intelligence to it. Try to get an American journalist to talk sensibly about the mental picture of politics on display in the news pages: the assumptions about political behavior, the understanding of what politics serves for, the nature of truth in the political sphere. The experience is deeply frustrating. Either the question is heard as an accusation of "bias" (Why don't you admit to having an agenda?), or it is dismissed as an "academic" inquiry, fit for a university seminar but irrelevant to daily practice. As Michael Janeway put it, "We are not in the philosophy business."

This is a costly attitude in a field that admits to becoming more "interpretive." Listen to Joseph Lelyveld, executive editor of the *New York Times*, talking about the growing need for journalists to interpret the news:

> People have a lot of facts in their heads when they turn to the morning newspaper, and it is only logical that they look for perspective, interpretation and serious thinking. . . . I think we carry the same burdens of fairness that we always carried, but there is a higher priority on saying what is really going on here.[29]

Lelyveld's "higher priority" makes sense; we do want journalists to help us make sense of the world. The difficulty is that there are innumerable ways to do "serious thinking" about the day's events. If the president gives a State of the Union address, one can think seriously about the speech as a work of rhetoric, where rhetoric is understood as a noble political art. An equally serious thinker can approach the speech as a political ploy likely to have this or that effect. For such a thinker, "rhetoric" is what covers over the politics of the matter. A third journalist-thinker, serious to the core, can place the speech in a historical context, where it resonates with previous speeches or earlier events. But the context may be the current political season, the Clinton era, the television age, the postwar world, the American republic. None of these interpretive strategies is obvious or inherent in events. They are choices made in the mind of the interpreter.

To take an example, R. W. Apple of the *New York Times* interpreted Bill Clinton's 1995 State of the Union speech in an article the paper classified as "news analysis":

> The State of the Union Message that the President delivered tonight was notably short on demands for action and long on appeals for comity—a demonstration of just how much he has weakened in the last 12 months.

Then, he was on the offensive, promising change as broad
as it was bold. He attacked those, like Senator Bob Dole of
Kansas, now the majority leader, who supported incremen-
tal change in health care. Now, he is on the defensive,
proposing nothing remotely resembling the revolution that
he and Hillary Rodham Clinton once espoused: instead, he
called for gradualism à la Dole.[30]

This brand of "serious thinking" proceeds from certain assumptions. According to Apple, what matters about most events in
Washington is the clues they offer to an all-important question: How
can we estimate the president's current political standing within
Beltway power circles? Is the president going to be perceived as
strong and intimidating or will he appear weak and "on the defensive"? What emerges as his "analysis" depends entirely on Apple's
habitual way of seeing, in which political reality is assumed to coin-
cide with current perceptions among insiders in Washington. Of
course, there is no way to separate those perceptions from the craft-
ing of perception on the front page of the *New York Times*, and in
this sense Apple is performing as an actor, accomplishing what he
claims to be analyzing.

None of this is lost on people in Washington. But all of it is invisible to an intellectual tradition that simply has no language for what
Apple is doing. Words like "analysis" and "interpretation" don't begin
to describe it because they say nothing about the thought work that
precedes the analysis and gives rise to the interpretation. Why does
Apple ask whether the president is "weakening" and "on the defensive"? What makes this a useful analytical frame, especially when compared to its alternatives? Here is one alternative from Tony Wharton,
a staff writer for the *Virginian-Pilot* in Norfolk, a paper at the forefront
of public journalism. Wharton examined the same Clinton speech and
found something else going on.

In urging Americans to become better citizens Tuesday night,
President Bill Clinton touched on an issue that cuts to the
core of democracy and potentially to the credibility of his
presidency.

"Our civil life is suffering," Clinton said near the beginning of the State of the Union speech to Congress. "Citizens
are working together less, shouting at each other more. The
common bonds of community which have been the great
strength of this country from its beginning are badly frayed."

Clinton's theme is one that is being discussed by a widening circle, but until Tuesday it was largely confined to academia and think tanks.

In a nutshell, the question being considered is this: Is democracy most at risk from the inside, because . . . too many are acting more out of self-interest than the common good, because people simply don't know their neighbors?

Americans should shoulder their civic responsibilities and have the courage to act for the common good, Clinton said. The question, some on the forefront of the debate wonder, is whether he can follow through as well.[31]

Here, the analysis takes Clinton's rhetoric about civic life seriously, as a way of holding him accountable for appropriate "follow-through." It focuses not on the president's "weakness" among insiders in Washington, but the potential strength he lent to a discussion about democracy that had previously been confined to educated circles. By listening for different cues, bringing a different set of expectations to the speech, Wharton emerges with a different "analysis."

Analysis must be grounded in something—especially if, as Lelyveld suggests and other studies confirm, it looms larger than ever in the news.[32] While the ideas that gave rise to any work of journalistic analysis can often be deduced, they are rarely discussed. Even more rarely are they defended, in part because the very idea seems to violate the doctrine of "objectivity."

Objectivity can mean many things in journalism.[33] The disinterested pursuit of truth, the care to ground reporting in verifiable facts, the principled attempt to restrain one's own biases and avoid prejudice are core values from which the press draws practical guidance and moral strength. No one should trifle with them. But objectivity also has its weaknesses. Under its influence "facts" tend to be placed in one category, "opinions" or personal views in another; with this division the journalist's mind appears to be successfully mapped. This works for some purposes: the facts about, say, a dispute in Congress over abortion can be separated from personal opinion on the issue; and every good reporter knows what it means to obey this scruple.

But there is a whole category of intellectual work that eludes the language of objectivity, with its attendant concerns about "bias." I have mentioned the mental pictures that point journalists in the direction of some facts, and away from others—like the image of Washington politics as a game of perception in which the president is either "gaining momentum" or "on the defensive." Now is that a fact or an opinion?

Clearly, it is neither. It is a way of seeing, a kind of mental equipment, that generates facts and occasions opinions. But suppose this equipment is faltering and needs to be replaced. Suppose, in other words, that "politics as a Washington perception game" has outlived its usefulness? Objectivity, despite its merits, leaves journalism without resources for naming and addressing such a problem. It extracts an intellectual cost that over time can amount to a defect in the journalist's self-understanding.

Bill Kovach, who formerly headed the Washington bureau for the *New York Times*, reflected on these costs in describing what he called "cold war journalism," typified by a unconscious use of cold war categories and images. About the reporting on the Balkan countries in the American press, Kovach observed:

> Everything written since World War II was informed by the "parables" of the East-West confrontation which have guided our foreign policy debates through Republican and Democratic Administrations for the past 40 years. Every country in the region was viewed through a cold war prism by diplomats, by political and social leaders, by academic institutions, and by journalists.
>
> From this perspective none of the countries in the region was described or understood in its own context or the context of its relationship to its neighbors. Each was fit into the parable of the cold war—robbed of its own identity or importance. As a result it is difficult, if not impossible, to adequately understand or describe the forces which now buffet and shape the region.[34]

As Kovach shows, mental devices like "prisms" and "parables" can shape (or misshape) an entire genre of reporting. But they tend to escape notice within the daily culture of journalism.

This much ought to be evident: to peer at the world through journalism is to see certain things highlighted for us—cold war conflict, for example—while others are not. Journalists have their own way of seeing, a lens on the world, just as doctors, social workers, and political consultants do. As things stand, however, discussions of how that lens works and how it might be improved are short-circuited by an official doctrine that states, "We have no lens. Or if we do, it is only on the editorial page." Or, as editors typically assert, if the lens is labeled "news analysis," then the reader has been told what to expect.[35] Whether such un-intellectual attitudes can still be afforded when "analysis" and "interpretation" are on the rise is a question serious minds in the press need to face.

But the larger problem is this: The language of professional journalism is not a rich language to think with, which is troubling because it prevents a creative response to all the alarms detailed here.

* * *

These, then, are the alarm bells that are ringing simultaneously:

Economic: It is not clear what journalism produces that has enough added value to sustain serious practice.

Technological: Journalism holds an uncertain place in a reconfigured world where information will be everywhere.

Political: Public support is badly eroded because the press is implicated in a political system that doesn't work.

Occupational: Newsrooms need to become exciting and innovative places that are more democratic and more diverse; professional standards need to be upheld.

Spiritual: We don't know what journalists are willing to be "for," so familiar are they with what they're "against."

Intellectual: It is difficult to think well with the existing language of journalism and thus address all these other issues.

Of course, this is only one way of describing the scene; others might tell a different tale. Before I explain how public journalism responds to these developments, I want to consider an alternative explanation for the troubles in the press—one that is popular with many working journalists.

This story notes with alarm the commercialization of the news formula, the rise of "tabloid television" and its creeping influence on the serious press, the marketing ethic that threatens to overtake the newsroom, the "bottom-line" mentality that seems everywhere in evidence. These disturbing trends are commonly interpreted as the degradation of "public service" traditions in the press. According to this view, journalism once thrived because owners and managers had more scruples. They understood that producing the news was a business unlike any other, "a sacred trust to be guarded in the public interest," in the words of James Squires, former editor of the *Chicago Tribune.*

Now those values are said to be gone. Executives who run newsrooms today are interested only in money matters—largely because they have to answer to Wall Street. They don't care about the quality of the journalism being done. They care about ratings, circulation figures, and demographics; they are obsessed with cost cutting to improve quarterly earnings. The result is more pandering to the lowest common denominator, more dubious innovations inspired by product marketing, and less investment in serious news gathering. In brief, journalism is dying because its corporate sponsors are killing it. Squires, an articulate promoter of this view, writes of the "willful destruction of the journalistic soul that had always made the press a business different from the rest."[36] The destroyer is the soulless corporation and its agents.

In my travels through the American press I have encountered many variations on this depressing theme from journalists who themselves seem depressed. My sympathies are with them. Those who uphold public service over corporate greed are undoubtedly on the right side of the issue. But their righteousness—I did not say self-righteousness—is also part of the problem. The headline, "Greedy Media Moguls Degrade and Defund the Press" is no vengeful fantasy; as Squires shows, it fits a good many facts. But there is one fact it fails to acknowledge: Unless they desire to fade away, journalists need a more constructive analysis of their predicament, one that illuminates their own contribution to the problem, prepares them to respond, identifies common ground with others who value the press and do not want to see its demise, points them in the direction of useful reforms, and restores a sense of mission and hope.

Public journalism is one attempt to tell this more productive tale. It has a great distance to travel before it succeeds; there is every chance that the young movement will be marginalized by the rest of the press or defeated by its own failure to mature and grow. But even that prospect is better than a victimology that leaves journalists inert and demoralized.

At the 1995 conference of Investigative Reporters and Editors, a leading professional organization, I joined in a panel discussion on public journalism. Expecting the usual criticisms, I was startled to hear myself challenged by an audience member who suggested that perhaps he and his colleagues "shouldn't exist." Newspaper journalism had run its course, he said; talk of reform was beside the point, a sentimental dialogue with the near-dead. I mumbled a brief reply, but in truth I was baffled: What does one say to a "challenger" who insists on his own demise? In a similar vein, Leonard Downie has remarked on how "many people in our profession seem to be giving up," turning the news pages "into replicas of television," rather than strengthening editorial quality.[37]

This gets to the heart of the problem, for reinvesting in quality journalism is more difficult than it seems. Persuading tightfisted managers to loosen their budgets and show more patience during cyclical ups and downs may be part of it. But equally important is for journalists to reckon with the drift of their craft in recent years, the qualities lent to the news through the residue of their own practices, the assertion of their own values. Especially worrisome is the development described by Marvin Kalb, the longtime correspondent for CBS and NBC, as "a disconnect between the press and the public it is supposed to serve." Echoing many other observers, Kalb notes how "the press seems absorbed by process while the public yearns for a serious exploration of the issues."[38]

This divide can no longer be ignored. And that is where public journalism gets to work. By addressing itself to the "disconnect," the movement tries to make journalists actors in their predicament, rather than victims of the media industry's narrow priorities, bystanders to the public's growing disaffection with the press, or passengers aboard a professional ship gone adrift.

4/THE ORIGINS OF
PUBLIC JOURNALISM

A description of three early projects—two at the *Wichita Eagle*, one at the *Charlotte Observer*—will show how the origins of public journalism lay in a creative response to the dangers of the "disconnect." Both papers are owned by Knight-Ridder, Inc., whose chief executive at the time, James K. Batten, had spoken eloquently on the need for newspapers to address the "sluggish state of civic health in many communities."[1] Batten saw "community connectedness" as a possible meeting ground between public service traditions in the press and the business imperatives of a struggling industry. Among those who responded was Davis Merritt, editor of the *Wichita Eagle* and a thirty-five-year veteran of the newspaper world.

Like many of his colleagues, Merritt was disgusted by the spectacle the nation endured during the 1988 presidential campaign. Shortly after the election, he wrote a column calling for "a total rearranging of the contract between the candidates and journalists." The existing arrangement, a "mutual bond of expediency," was satisfying only to the campaign professionals who had learned how to profit from it. Merritt fixed on the false sense of motion the system produced. As the campaign went forward, public dialogue did not progress, despite daily coverage of what the candidates did and said. Of the campaign consultants' approach he wrote:

> While your man is standing still, make sure he says nothing of substance. Then say something pungent but pointless, preferably about the opponent, and jump on a bus or plane for the next stop. The trailing pack of journalists has no choice but to hastily rip out a new lead or a sound-bite and

34

race for the next stop, fearful, despite all recent evidence to
the contrary, that something meaningful might occur on the
next tarmac or courthouse square.[2]

These were standard observations about the manipulation of the
campaign press. What made them interesting was Merritt's emphasis
on a "new political contract" that he said journalists would have to
initiate. In the 1990 gubernatorial campaign in Kansas, the *Eagle* did
just that. Sensing a repeat of the pattern of 1988—a campaign of phony
charges and countercharges with only minimal attention to important issues—Merritt announced a break with tradition in a Sunday
column headlined, "Up Front, Here's Our Election Bias."

The headline was itself noteworthy: a news organization shares its
plans with the public by announcing the "bias" it will bring to campaign coverage. Of course, the particular slant Merritt had in mind
was hardly controversial. ("We believe the voters are entitled to have
the candidates talk about the issues in depth." Few would dare to challenge that.) But making good on this pledge involved a significant shift
in the premise of campaign journalism. The notion of "covering the
campaign" was effectively replaced by a new principle: making the
campaign "cover" what mattered to citizens. The *Eagle* vowed to give
readers "the opportunity to understand in great detail the candidates'
positions on every major issue Kansas faces."

This had important implications. It meant that the point of departure for the *Eagle* would no longer be the daily events along the campaign trail, or what the candidates were doing to win votes. It would be
the needs of citizens, who had a "right to know what the candidates
intend to do once in office."[3] Campaign coverage would approach the
candidates with this priority in mind. It was as if doctors, locked in a
battle with lawyers about who was more responsible for soaring mal-
practice costs, suddenly turned to patients to understand anew their
dissatisfactions with medical treatment. The *Eagle*'s "new political
contract" was novel only because it departed from what had become
the norm; in essence it was a return to fundamentals.

Merritt had recognized a simple fact about campaign journalism:
although the journalist's working relationship was with politicians and
their hired hands, the ultimate "client" was the public. His announcement carried another implication: If the *Eagle* was going to focus on
"every major issue Kansas faces," then defining those issues would
have to become the newspaper's responsibility. It could not be left to
the campaigns since the whole purpose of Merritt's approach was to
take the momentum away from the pollsters and handlers.

In effect, then, the *Eagle* was planning to argue with the campaigns over what "the campaign" should be about. Such a move could be seen as a naked power grab or the assumption of a deeper responsibility. Merritt was betting on his and his staff's knowledge of Kansas politics and their professional judgment. They had polling data to help them decide which issues were important to the people of the state, but this data still had to be interpreted, raising the question: What were the grounds for determining the central issues in the campaign?

For a campaign adviser, the answer is clear. A good issue is one that solidifies a base of support, motivates new recruits, weakens an opponent's coalition, or targets an important subgroup—typically, undecided voters. A bad issue is one that angers supporters, alienates potential recruits, or exposes a weakness in the candidate's record. The image of a "wedge" issue—one that divides the electorate to one side's advantage—suggests the values at work when campaign professionals do the naming and framing of issues.[4]

One way a journalist can counter those values is to reveal the candidate's strategy. The wedge and how it works may then become the object of "analysis." But think for a moment: how does this help me form my judgments as an intelligent person aware of the Kansas governor's race? Should I vote for the candidate with the best strategy? Reporters who try the expose the machinations of politicians and handlers believe they are striking a blow for truth, and they are, in a "buyer beware" manner typical of consumer reporting. But Merritt wanted the *Eagle*'s journalism to be more than a prophylactic, a series of signs reading "Beware of Manipulation by Candidates Trying to Win." Consider, then, two different ways of telling the story of the governor's race: one assumes that a campaign has its own reality, which journalists ought to decipher for us; the other assumes that the campaign becomes decipherable by us when it addresses the realities facing residents. The *Eagle* decided to strike its own blow for truth with the proposition that "voters are entitled to have the candidates talk about the issues in depth."

Supported by polling results, the *Eagle* focused its coverage on ten concerns: education, economic development, environment, agriculture, social services, abortion, crime, health care, taxes, and state spending.[5] Each was the subject of a long background piece in the Sunday paper. Each was also charted regularly in "Where They Stand," a weekly feature that gave a brief description of what was at stake, a summary of the two gubernatorial candidates' positions on the focal issues, and then a report on what, if anything, was said regarding those issues by the campaigns that week. For example, the section on the environment noted that Kansas faces new demands on its water supply as current sources dry up. Finding innovative ways to reuse water was a major concern throughout the state. The paper treated the positions of the two candidates (Democrat Joan Finney and incumbent Republican Mike Hayden) as follows:

FINNEY
Would increase the state's role in recycling. Has no specific plan. Has not discussed the water issue.
This week: Restated her position.

HAYDEN
Helped pass state water plan to manage resources. Wants private lands more accessible for public recreation. Encourages dryland farming research to reduce demand for water. Wants to research drilling wells into geological formations deeper than the Ogallala aquifer.
This week: Repeated his position.

Under the heading of "Agriculture," the *Eagle* had this to say about the Democrat:

FINNEY
Wants agriculture secretary elected by all voters. No other stated position on agricultural matters.
This week: Did not talk about it.

When "news" made was made under this format it tended to be news of positions taken or views clarified. For example, under the heading of "Taxes," the *Eagle* wrote:

FINNEY
Now is proposing that $460 million be raised by placing a 1 percent surcharge tax on up to 52 categories of goods and services now exempt from sales taxes. Finney would use the money to provide for a 30 percent reduction in property taxes.
This week: Substantially changed her tax proposal Tuesday. Originally had proposed raising $800 million in new tax dollars by placing a 1 percent surcharge tax on up to 52 categories of goods and services now exempt from sales tax. On Tuesday, she lowered that amount to $460 million. Would not say before the election which categories would be taxed.

Would use the money to provide for 30 percent reduction in property taxes. Would no longer raise $180 million for state programs—money she has said was necessary to deal with a possible state revenue shortfall.[6]

Several things are worth noting about this scheme. First, any responsible newspaper would report a major change in a candidate's position on taxes. In this sense the *Eagle*'s coverage was entirely conventional. What was different was the conscious display of issues and positions as the major theme of the campaign. If the pages of the newspaper are thought of as a public space designed by journalists, then what the *Eagle* did is arrange this space so that the proper concerns of politics ("issues in depth") shone through. Time was also reconceived. "This week: Did not talk about it" is a fact generated by a particular way of imagining political time: as the weekly process by which the choices facing the state are (or are not) discussed by the candidates. The strategy theme contains its own conception of time: how the candidates are shaping their images, outmaneuvering each other, struggling to win as the "race" winds down.

"Where They Stand" was thus more than a handy voter's guide, although it was also that. Fundamentally, it was an argument for what politics is supposed to be about: public concerns and public debate. It was a powerful use of political space, especially the threat of a blank appearing under a candidate's name. Deploying this threat was the *Eagle*'s way of being "tough" on the candidates. Here, however, toughness doesn't become an end in itself, as so often happens in political reporting. A candidate could avoid the penalty of white space by cooperating in a process that helps voters make up their minds. The journalist thus creates a system of incentives with clear rules for political speakers, who are rewarded for taking the risk of genuine public dialogue and punished for declining it.

Such a system, conscientiously deployed, offers an alternative to both the excesses of the adversarial pose, where a contemptuous dismissal of all public statements is assumed to serve some public good, and the limitations of "balance," in which equivalent quotes from opposite sides is the desired norm.[7] The *Eagle*'s approach, unlike these others, does discriminate, but on a principle that is announced and defensible: political speech should address our most important public concerns.

However, the public's immediate concerns may not include everything that is of genuine political concern. Starting with citizens' preoccupations, the *Eagle* had to take care to avoid being bound by them. It could not assume, for example, that candidates would neglect to go beyond "the issues," displaying vision and enterprise, to speak to deeper truths—deeper, perhaps, than people presently want to hear. The challenge to the *Eagle* was to remain open to this possibility, and to keep in mind that citizens are not gods, their vision not unfailing. Political reporting cannot be reduced to a restatement of their concerns. But surely it can begin there, which was the point of the *Eagle*'s experiment: to address the "disconnect" between public concerns and political dialogue.

Merritt's answer was a redirection of the newspaper's various and subtle powers—for example, the power to name and frame public issues, to view events through a particular lens, to arrange public space and define public time. These are forms of power journalists routinely deploy but rarely discuss. The *Eagle* learned to become self-conscious about them in order to alter their use; in the process it also redefined what campaign journalism was "for." Not a savvy take on a degrading spectacle but a useful handle on problems and choices is what the *Eagle* aimed to provide.

In a postelection survey financed by Knight-Ridder, readers said that the most useful features of campaign reporting were the "Where They Stand" box and the in-depth explorations of issues. "Horse race" coverage, often touted by journalists as a way to make the story exciting, ranked far down the list.[8]

A further (and more radical) experiment came two years later when the *Eagle* launched the "People Project."[9] It drew upon the insight that the troubles with politics (and journalism) went far deeper than elections and campaign coverage. Politics seemed not to address people's problems, and this meant that political journalism could not connect either, unless it revised its view of what politics was about. A definition built around government institutions was troublesome if these institutions were seen as out of touch or unable to solve problems. Ignoring government was no solution. But neither could journalists avoid the widespread frustration with politics-as-usual, or the growing conviction that some problems are beyond government's capacity or domain.

The "People Project" tried to respond by revivifying politics as a participatory drama. The experiment had a self-conscious and idealistic premise, namely, that journalism could "empower people to take back control of their lives," as Merritt's initial planning memo read. The project began with 192 two-hour interviews with Wichita area residents, who were asked to speak about their lives, troubles, and fears, along with their perceptions of the political process. From these interviews, and from the *Eagle*'s own observations, the following conclusions emerged, as outlined in the memo:

1. People feel alienated from many of the processes that affect their lives. The political process, the education system, the justice system are seen as incapable of resolving anything.

2. People see these issues as interrelated, inseparable and, perhaps, unsolvable.

3. People's response is to fall into frustration and anger, to drop out of the processes, to abandon community in a self-protective response, rather than seek solutions which they very much doubt exist.

Merritt was searching for a way to tackle public cynicism and despair without adding to it, on the one hand, or whitewashing reality, on the other. From one perspective, the idea that citizens can "take back control" of institutional structures and social forces seems naïve, perhaps dangerously so. It can lead to a kind of mythmaking, where the realities of power and influence are obscured by the charged rhetoric of "empowerment." Nonetheless, journalists have every reason to emphasize the citizen's ability to act, to take seriously the notion of "self-government" as the living root of democracy. A journalism so "realistic" that it sees through everything risks persuading people that politics is a farce, government a joke, rhetoric a sham, leadership an illusion, change a mirage. This is a journalism that *by succeeding* becomes defeatist and self-canceling. For if all these things are true, there is no need for journalists and their daily reports. Indeed, we have no use for democratic politics because problems and systems are clearly beyond our control.

It was just this fear—that public problems have gotten beyond us—that came through in the background interviews the *Eagle* conducted. In trying to counter despair, the "People Project" was not a utopian exercise at all, but a clear-eyed probing for a way to restore journalism's relevance. Merritt outlined the aims of his project as follows:

1. Recognize the frustrations and explain the reasons for them, including the core, often competing values that stand in the way of solutions.

2. Give readers hundreds of places where they can get a handle on problems through the existing, non-government mechanisms.

3.   Elicit from readers, and print, their ideas for other mechanisms and solutions.

4.   Summarize it all and produce a . . . reprint that would be distributed to non-subscribers through various devices. . . .

5.   Encourage, or, with a partner, actively cause continued involvement at various levels.

The "People Project" became a package of articles, service features, community events, and forums for swapping ideas sponsored by the *Eagle* and two broadcast partners. Its purpose was to persuade Wichita that at least some public problems could be dealt with, and not necessarily through the government. Accordingly, the subtitle of the project was "Solving It Ourselves." In a front-page column Merritt described the initiative as a "collaborative effort to give shape and momentum to your voices and ideas, with the goal of reasserting personal power and responsibility for what goes on around us." For ten weeks, Merritt wrote, the *Eagle* and its two partners, KSNW-TV and KNSS radio, would make the space and time available for "an informed community discussion of critical issues" from which "ideas about solutions can arise, as well as the commitment to carry out the solutions."

The "critical issues" emerged during background interviews as those most troubling to area residents. They included faltering schools, crime and the lure of gangs, political gridlock, and the stresses that built up on families and individuals trying to cope with competing demands. Each issue was the subject of a series of features in the *Eagle*, the bulk of them written by veteran reporter and longtime Wichita resident Jon Roe. Roe outlined the problem and what residents said about it in interviews; then he examined why the issue was so difficult to handle, attempting to cut through the surface of conflict and encouraging readers to examine their deepest values, as well as those of others that might challenge their own.

For each of the major issues under discussion, the *Eagle* published a comprehensive list called "Places to Start," with the names, addresses, and phone numbers of organizations and agencies working on the problem. Repeated invitations were made to readers to phone, write, fax, or deliver in person their comments and suggestions for change. A series of "idea exchanges" were held at various public sites, where concerned residents could link up with others like themselves and meet with representatives of community and volunteer groups.

A regular feature called "Success Stories" focused on individuals who took the initiative and were making a difference. The paper's broadcast partners produced parallel reports during the project's run and provided on-air forums for discussion.

The "People Project" was political journalism in a different key. The emphasis shifted from government and its contending factions to citizens themselves. The aim was to connect people with each other and to public life and its full range of voluntary organizations. The "People Project" drew on a long tradition of political thought, usually called civic republicanism, in which the ideal citizen is engaged with others through a rich web of local ties. Visiting the United States in the 1830s, Alexis de Tocqueville called these groups "associations"; for him they represented the tensile strength of American democracy.

"At the heart of republicanism," writes E. J. Dionne, "is the belief that self government is not a drab necessity but a joy to be treasured. It is the view that politics is not simply a grubby confrontation of competing interests but an arena in which citizens can learn from each other and discover an 'enlightened self-interest' in common."[10] By portraying Wichita as a civic culture rich with opportunities for mutual engagement, the *Eagle* made use of a power that is rarely visible in discussions of the press: the ability to render the political landscape in a particular way; in this case, as inhabitable by concerned residents willing to learn from each other and "get involved." What were the results? As Merritt later wrote, "Kansas was not free of crime or health care problems and the schools did not visibly improve—nor had we anticipated any of that." There were a few hopeful signs. Volunteerism in Wichita schools was up 37 percent when the school year opened. Though newspaper circulation remained flat, as expected, in an annual survey by Knight-Ridder, reader satisfaction rose 10 percent, the highest increase in the chain.[11]

Both of the original Wichita projects recognized that beyond "information," the press sends out an *invitation* to experience public life in one manner or another. Expanding on what this invitation should say is the real innovation pioneered by Merritt and his colleagues. The experience should be participatory, the *Eagle* dared to assert. It should propose and deliver a useful dialogue about issues. It should address people in their capacity as citizens, in the hope of strengthening that capacity. It should try to make public life go well, in the sense of making good on democracy's promise. These "shoulds" would later form the core of public journalism as a philosophy. Merritt described the venture's results:

Something intriguing and promising had happened. We had deliberately broken out of the passive and increasingly detrimental conventions of election coverage. We had, in effect, left the press box and gotten down on the field, not as a contestant but as a fair-minded participant with an open and expressed interest in the process going well. . . . It was also a liberating moment, for me and the journalists at the Eagle. We no longer had to be the victims, along with the public, of a politics gone sour. We had a new purposefulness: revitalizing a moribund public process.[12]

In the fall of 1992, this "purposefulness" was taken further by the *Charlotte Observer* with a bold experiment in election coverage.[13] Like others in journalism, executive editor Rich Oppel was dissatisfied with press performance in past campaigns, particularly with horse race polling, which had miscalled a bitter 1990 Senate race between Jesse Helms and Harvey Gantt. That embarrassing episode had a "last straw" quality for the *Observer.* The weaknesses of horse race coverage were well-known; now its biggest strength, the ability to predict the winner, was also suspect.

In 1992, Oppel and publisher Rolfe Neill were determined to try something different. Meanwhile, the Poynter Institute for Media Studies, which has an educational mission within journalism, was looking to demonstrate that a revised approach was possible. Aware of the progress that had been made in the Wichita paper's 1990 election coverage, the two institutions agreed to cooperate, adding as a partner WSOC-TV, with which the paper had conducted joint polling in the past. The *Observer* set out to amplify and extend the "new political contract" outlined two years earlier by Merritt. In a front-page column entitled, "We'll Help You Regain Control of the Issues," Oppel announced the paper's intentions:

David Broder of the *Washington Post* has said voters see no "connection between their concerns in their daily lives and what they hear talked about and see reported by the press in most political campaigns."
We think this is dangerous. . . .
We will seek to reduce the coverage of campaign strategy and candidates' manipulations, and increase the focus on voters' concerns. We will seek to distinguish between issues that merely influence an election's outcome and those of governance that will be relevant after the election. We will

link our coverage to the voters' agenda, and initiate more questions on behalf of the voters.[14]

Oppel's column represents a kind of coming clean that was long overdue in campaign journalism. He admits that politics-as-strategy is a narrative device that ought to be drastically reduced; then he declares that his newspaper will be consciously applying a new "focus on voters' concerns." He acknowledges that the temporal frame—the definition of political time—that ordinarily shapes campaign coverage is too narrow, focusing as it does on "issues that merely influence an election's outcome." He then announces the choice of a new frame: matters of "governance that will be relevant after the election." He admits that question-asking is an important public function that can be performed several different ways. The way the *Observer* chooses is to "initiate more questions on behalf of the voters."

In the same passage, Oppel concedes that "covering politics" and "having an agenda" are not mutually exclusive; then he vows, "We will link our coverage to the voters' agenda." Finally, he declares that a newspaper inevitably has convictions about politics ("We think this is dangerous") and that news coverage *follows from those convictions* ("We'll help you regain control of the issues"). This is a far cry from traditional thinking in journalism, which pretends that convictions are properly "contained" within the editorial page, while the news pages remain uncontaminated by anything so messy and emotional. In short, Oppel's column recognizes that the design of political coverage is itself an issue to be discussed openly with the public.

The search for a "citizen's agenda" began in January of 1992 with a poll of one thousand adults (not necessarily readers) conducted by a Knight-Ridder subsidiary and jointly sponsored by WSOC-TV. The poll asked residents not who they would vote for, or what they wanted to read, but what they were concerned about and wanted the candidates to discuss in the upcoming election. Six broad areas of concern emerged: the economy and taxes, crime and drugs, health care, education, the environment, and a general sense that support structures and value systems in family and community life were weakening. These became the "citizen's agenda." Five hundred of the poll's respondents agreed to serve on a "citizen's panel" to help the *Observer* keep its focus on the public's concerns rather than the machinations of the candidates or the weekly flux of campaign events.

Issues from the citizen's agenda did dominate the subsequent coverage, with emphasis on answering questions, explaining the candidates' positions, and exploring possible solutions. Queries from citizens were regularly put to the candidates and campaign staffs; polls and strategy stories were downplayed. Stories were told through the eyes and lives of citizens, relying heavily on readers' phoned-in comments and questions from the citizen's panel. With the citizen's agenda driving the coverage, reporters specializing in business, education, health, and religion were recruited to write political stories, focusing on possible solutions as well as problems. Profiles of the candidates and their voting records and campaign speeches were "mapped" against the agenda.

Voters emerged as participants in the campaign. Reporters on the campaign trail would ask questions on behalf of individual readers; replies would be published under a regular heading, "Ask the Candidates." Before the state primary, Pat Buchanan was interviewed by eight members of the citizen's panel. Three panel members questioned gubernatorial candidates at a debate on school reform. For three Sunday evenings in October, WSOC-TV featured a televised conversation among citizens keyed to issues explored in the Sunday newspaper.

These events reveal another dimension of press power that ordinarily goes unnoticed: journalists determine who counts as a "player" in politics. As communication scholar Michael Schudson puts it, among the tools the press employs is the "capacity to publicly include."[15] Making use of this capacity, the *Observer* told a different story about the 1992 election: the story of citizens, candidates, and public concerns connecting with each other—or failing to connect.

The reorientation required an extraordinary effort. Virtually the entire staff from business reporters to feature writers contributed something to the revamped coverage. Space was increased. Coverage of the presidential race almost doubled over the previous campaign— some 18,000 square inches was provided compared with 10,500 in 1988. According to Poynter, issue coverage went from 1,890 square inches in 1988 (18 percent of the total campaign coverage) to 5,716 in 1992 (32 percent). Coverage of campaign strategy fell from 21 percent of total campaign coverage in 1988 to 11 percent in 1992; horse race polls declined from 6.1 percent to 1.4 percent. News of what the candidates did and said remained constant.[16]

Before the initiative began, Oppel said, "If we do campaign coverage this way, it will change the way we do everything here."[17] By making the citizen's experience the primary reference point, the paper began to alter fundamentally the way journalists viewed the political drama as well. The best illustration of this shift is a story told by Oppel from the 1992 campaign.

Voters were intensely interested in the environment. . . . So
our reporters went out to senatorial candidates and said,
"Here are the voters' questions." Terry Sanford, the incumbent senator, called me up from Washington and said, "Rich,
I have these questions from your reporter and I'm not going
to answer them because we are not going to talk about the
environment until the general election." This was the primary. I said, "Well, the voters want to know about the environment now, Terry." He said, "Well, that's not the way I
have my campaign structured." I said, "Fine, I will run the
questions and I will leave a space under it for you to answer.
If you choose not to, we will just say 'would not respond' or
we will leave it blank." We ended the conversation. In about
ten days he sent the answers down. . . .[18]

What this story illustrates is the intricate relations between power
and authority in political journalism. Clearly, Oppel was deploying
the power of his newspaper with his threat to leave a blank space
under Sanford's name. But he had other weapons on his side: the
renewed authority that came from the effective representation of citizens' interests, and from the legitimate attempt to make the campaign dialogue a discussion of important issues. The pre-election poll,
the newspaper's interviews with citizens, and the fact that readers
were constantly urged to phone, write and fax with questions and
comments gave teeth to the claim to be representing citizens. This
claim, always to some degree rhetorical, became more and more
empirical as the *Observer* found ways to define, then pursue, a "citizen's agenda." All of this helped to make the *Observer*'s power play an
instance of fair play.

Another intriguing dimension of Oppel's story involves what did
not happen. When Terry Sanford explained that his campaign strategy
did not include talking about the environment yet, Oppel did not say,
"Oh really? Tell me your thinking on that." This is the dark hole that
strategy stories tumble down. The journalist's curiosity is aroused by
the insinuation of a clever move, the effectiveness of which can only
be appreciated by a savvy observer, which is the kind journalists want
to be. "That's not the way I have my campaign structured" is a subtle
invitation to Oppel to enter the universe of handlers and pollsters. By
declining, Oppel stayed within the universe of citizen concerns. He also
let Sanford know how the *Observer* itself would be "structuring" the
campaign: as a dialogue on public issues. Like any good journalist, he

hung tough with Sanford as the senator tried to squirm away. But toughness was placed in the service of public dialogue.

Contrast this with the brand of toughness put forward by interrogators of President Bush during the 1992 campaign. As paraphrased by scholar Thomas Patterson, their questions were:

> You say you haven't been good at getting your message across, but don't the polls indicate a rejection of the message in and of itself?

> Hasn't the pattern of the primaries been such that the American people are looking for an alternative to you?

> You've put Pat Buchanan behind you, but isn't Perot the inheritor of the anti-Bush vote?[19]

This is the journalist's cult of "toughness" in action. The thrust of these questions is toward delegitimating the president's reelection campaign, to place before Bush (and the nation) the evidence that he is, or seems to be, a "loser." Of course, the more likely effect is to delegitimate the press, for such questions frequently lack any connection to the public's genuine interests. Presumably this is one reason 71 percent of Americans think the press "gets in the way of society solving its problems."

Glancing again at the "aggressive" questions listed above, imagine a phone call with the White House similar to Oppel's conversation with Sanford. Could any editor say, with a clear conscience and a convincing tone, that citizens want such "issues" treated as whether "the polls indicate a rejection of the message?" Would the editor threaten to leave a blank space under Bush's name if the president chose not to answer? Clearly not. But the *Observer* could and did print a series of questions from readers that the Bush campaign declined to answer.[20]

There is good reason, then, for any tough-minded political reporter to take seriously the notion of a "citizen's agenda." Absent the authority derived from the public's legitimate interest in serious discussion, the power of the press is not only less legitimate but less powerful. The public's "right to know" is ritually invoked; but it becomes a forceful claim only when attached to a reporting agenda that is persuasively "public," rather than narrowly professional.

The *Charlotte Observer*'s 1992 experiment sought a restoration of journalistic authority through a stronger connection to citizens and their deepest political concerns. Like the earlier initiatives at the Wichita *Eagle*, the experiment required journalists to lay hold of their power to imagine public life in a particular way, and to shape their reports accordingly. By becoming conscious of the design they were giving to political news—citizens as participants, politics as serious discussion—the journalists involved took a major step in improving that design. They began to address what Howard Kurtz called a "fatal disconnection, a growing gap between editors and reporters on the one hand and consumers of news on the other."

5/PUTTING CITIZENS AT THE CENTER

Journalists at the *Eagle* and the *Observer* did not call what they were doing "public journalism" when they launched their experiments. Nor did others who were thinking like thoughts and trying similar things. The term emerged later, around 1993, to describe a resemblance in approach among those in the press seeking a stronger bond with citizens, a more constructive role in public dialogue, or some way to contribute to problem solving at the local level.

Many of these early efforts sought to improve election coverage by developing and emphasizing a "citizen's agenda" or something similar. Others tried to create public forums where residents could join in discussions too often monopolized by experts and insiders. A few, like the "People Project," addressed citizens as potential actors, employing the newspaper as a kind of motivational tool, a guide and goad to public engagement. All took aim at the disconnect between the press and public.

During the period 1990 to 1993, I began to learn of these initiatives and to discuss them with the editors involved. I was struck by their still-evolving but hopeful assumptions about democracy, journalism and political life. The following seemed to be key:

1. Politics and public life are open to all, and journalists should learn to present them that way.

2. Democracy requires "information," supplied by the press as a matter of course, but it also demands "participation," which the press can invite.

3. Journalism at its best addresses people in their capacity as responsible citizens—not as idle consumers, thrill-seeking spectators, or powerless victims.

4.   Politics should involve public problem solving, preceded by
     reflection and discussion. By learning to see it this way, the press
     can begin to appreciate and address the public's frustration with
     the political system.

5.   "Discussion" is not the same thing as "debate." There is plenty
     of debate, but too little of it makes room for citizens or makes
     sense to them as a means of reaching solutions. Missing are
     opportunities for "deliberative" dialogue, in which people sort
     through difficulties, reflect on choices, listen with care, and deep-
     en their views. Such talk is not beyond the reach of most people,
     although it is rare in their experience. Making it less rare is a legit-
     imate goal of the press.

6.   The values journalists hold inform their work. A different jour-
     nalism would likely result from a deeper concern for civic partic-
     ipation, public problem solving, deliberative dialogue, and the
     integrity of public life.

In *Politics for People*, David Mathews, president of the Kettering
Foundation, outlines the view of political life that came to animate
many of the best experiments. Citizens "are the primary officeholders in a democracy," Mathews notes.

> Democratic politics doesn't begin in voting to create gov-
> ernment; it begins in the choices about what kind of com-
> munity and country people want. The most basic form of
> politics is conversation about these choices and about what
> is really in the public's interest. Serious public discourse is
> the seedbed, the wellspring of democratic politics because
> only the public can define the public's interest. The quality of
> democracy depends on the quality of this kind of public talk.
> Changing the quality of the public dialogue [thus] begins to
> change politics.[1]

If taken seriously by an increasing number of journalists, observations like these might develop into a kind of public philosophy for a
reenergized press. The Project on Public Life and the Press, launched
in 1993 by the Kettering Foundation (which sponsored some early discussions on the theme), the Knight Foundation, American Press
Institute and New York University, was designed to pursue this possibility.[2] By compiling information about the various experiments under

way, by bringing together those conducting them for seminars and workshops, by developing with the journalists involved a vocabulary they could employ as they continued their efforts, and taking the whole discussion on the road to sites where journalists were debating their future, the Project would seek to open a space within the press where "journalism" could be imagined differently. "Public" or "civic" journalism is really a name for that discussion, which is supported by other institutions, most notably the Pew Center for Civic Journalism, funded by the Pew Charitable Trusts and directed by veteran broadcast journalist Edward Fouhy.

By 1995 public journalism had been tried in one form or another at more than one hundred and fifty news organizations; it was a major topic of discussion in professional circles. This was gratifying for a notion that had only a tiny foothold a few years earlier. But such a sudden rise brought trouble with it. The version of public journalism that has been popularized throughout the press is superficial enough to permit all kinds of abuse, not only by critics but by enthusiasts as well. As the experiments continue, some will prove disappointing, while others may strike even sympathetic observers as misguided. They may make a perfunctory stab at consulting "real folks" without demanding much from them. Glib claims about finding "the people's voice" are already too prominent in the movement, lending support to skeptics who sense another exercise in media hype. In a nation still addicted to the romance of small-town democracy, a few hastily gathered "town meetings" can pass as a serious civic exercise. There is a strong temptation to label such token efforts "public journalism."

One day in 1994, I received a call from a reporter at the *San Jose Mercury News*, who wanted to inform me of the paper's latest civic journalism initiative. It turned out to be an effort to improve voter participation in a district where a high percentage of immigrants was cited as contributing to a chronically low turnout. The project sounded wrongheaded and even dangerous to me, because it singled out a particular population. Why favor one district over another, courting charges of undue interference in the election? The reporter was clearly wounded that the man he had phoned, a self-described champion of public journalism, had no praise and little constructive advice. Nonetheless, the project went forward, and "public journalism" took some well-deserved knocks in the San Jose newsroom.

I sometimes wonder if the idea of public journalism can survive its worst examples, which are doubtless still to come. The only antidote, I believe, is that a nuanced understanding must be spread to more and more of the working press, so that journalists can apply high standards to anything they hear presented as public journalism. This is one reason the poor quality of the debate today is so troubling. It is based on a crude caricature of an idea that needs to be grasped at its deeper levels if it is to avoid turning into mush.

Tom Still, associate editor of the *Wisconsin State Journal* in Madison, describes public journalism as "a group of recovering traditional journalists, who have come to believe that their profession is at least partly responsible for the sense of alienation that pervades America's political culture."[3] His newspaper is active in one of the movement's most productive partnerships, "We the People/Wisconsin," which includes Wisconsin Public Television and Radio, WISC-TV in Madison, a commercial station, and the Pew Center, which provides some funding.[4]

Initially, the Madison partners sought to take advantage of joint primary dates in Wisconsin and Minnesota to lure 1992 presidential candidates to the area for a televised debate. But the venture quickly took a wider aim: to "address the fact that we have democracy without deliberation," as Still put it. The "We the People" project places citizens on the public stage as participants and demands of them serious examination of issues that matter to them. Along with election forums that give ordinary folk a much larger role in questioning candidates have come a mock legislative panel where citizens wrestled with the reform of property taxes and took testimony from state legislators, a citizen's "jury" that examined costs and trade-offs of various health care plans, a young people's political caucus that brought youths together from around the state for an assessment of politics from their perspective, and a discussion of government deficits that plunged participants into the details of a problem long considered the province of insiders and academics.

The inspiration for "We the People" is clearly the American jury system, which assumes the ability of people from any background to deliberate and reach a decision. Preceded by as many as six "town meetings" on the chosen topic across the state and by extensive news coverage that focuses squarely on the issue at hand, the Wisconsin forums try to showcase informed dialogue among citizens in preparation for the display of opinion and the questioning of officials. In this sense their goal is to model for a statewide audience the forms of talk that make public dialogue something more than a shouting match or gripe session. If this sounds like a prescription for boring television, consider that several "We the People" broadcasts have been ratings hits—including one on land use that easily that won its time period (7:00 P.M.) with a 25 percent share of the viewing audience.[5]

GETTING THE CONNECTIONS RIGHT

By erecting and maintaining a public forum where deliberation is the rule, the Madison partnership has offered citizens of the state a new political resource. An immediate payoff came during the 1994 governor's campaign, when a citizen rose to request from each candidate a detailed plan to reform property taxes—in writing, he said, and at least two weeks before the election. Facing a live statewide audience, the candidates promised to comply—and they did. Neither had released such particulars before.

The Madison partnership is about more than giving voice to people. A deeper purpose is to reconfigure the political drama so that it more often centers on citizens and their concerns; in the process, political journalism gets redefined as well. This happens in a direct and visible way when, for example, citizens occupy a hearing room in the Wisconsin state capitol. Sitting where their representatives sit, amid the glare of the television cameras, they may quiz a state legislator who is "testifying" to them about tax policy or health care. A startling visual of this sort can easily become a gimmick, of course. But the potential for misuse only underlines its importance. Television news traffics in symbols as a matter of routine: the correspondent who stands in front of the state capitol for a live report borrows the state-house to authenticate what follows. When decisions are made about the use of such symbols, which priorities should prevail? The Wisconsin experiment has an answer to that question: priority should go to deliberation on common problems; citizens should be featured because they are the "primary officeholders." A journalism that does equal justice to these convictions and to the realities of politics is what the partnership is trying to create.

In one "We the People" forum, the focus was on a Wisconsin state supreme court election, a race that ordinarily draws meager attention and low turnout. Under these circumstances, politics becomes a game of insiders. Judicial candidates view the state bar association and the trial lawyers' groups as the de facto electorate and tailor their campaigns accordingly. A journalism that accepts the proposition that "politics is about winners and losers" would naturally focus on the endorsement derby among candidates. Reporters might attend the bar association forum and try to discern who "won." After all, are these backroom maneuvers not what the election is about? No, said the Madison partners. The election is about the people of Wisconsin and a state court that will decide important matters of public interest.

About seventy citizen volunteers from around the state were recruited to participate in the forum. They were given a discussion guide, prepared by the partnership, that explained what the court does and some of the questions that might come before the judges. They then deliberated for several hours about the questions they had and the concerns they wanted to raise with the candidates. The televised forum, held in the court's chambers, featured seven of these people questioning the two major-party candidates, who were placed in the position of trial lawyers pleading their case. The remaining volunteers sat in the audience, watching their peers conduct the inquiry.

The emphasis on deliberation in the Madison forums shapes the journalism the partners do beforehand. Political reporting gets redefined as preparation for the ensuing discussion. Thus, the *State Journal* published a job description for a supreme court judge (a "bit of a civics lesson," according to Still) and highlighted the issues likely to come before the court that might matter to Wisconsin residents. "This election is ordinarily a popularity contest within the legal community," Still explained. "We tried to open it up."

For ex-reporters like Still, civic journalism is a response to the frustrations of routine government watching: "I had written one too many stories that began, 'The subcommittee voted 4 to 3 yesterday . . . ,' then watched as the full committee reversed the vote, and the entire house reversed the committee." Defining politics as what happens within the walls of government creates a problem when government is seemingly unable to address common concerns. Coming to grips with this failure means questioning the basis for what journalists call "news judgment." Still said, "We need to quit substituting our judgment about what's on people's minds for listening to what is actually there." This simple switch—to active listening as the starting point for news coverage—is one way of addressing the disconnection so apparent to Still and many of his colleagues.

Among them is John Dinges, editorial director of National Public Radio and the driving force behind NPR's 1994 election project. The project featured partnerships matching NPR stations to local newspapers for various Charlotte-style efforts. A key principle in the NPR program was to introduce journalists to the notion of deliberative dialogue, where people reflect on the choices they face rather than simply express themselves. By training journalists in what a deliberative discussion is, by experimenting with public forums and citizen panels that were more deliberative in character than the typical "town meeting," NPR stations and their print partners sought to inject a more thoughtful public voice into their election reporting—something beyond the stereotypical angry voter demanding "change."[6]

Dinges started thinking about a different approach after he learned of the *Charlotte Observer*'s 1992 project. "Following the rules of straight journalism was not fulfilling the role I thought we should be playing," he said. "Giving our analysis, digging out the dirt, being the watchdog—these were leading us into a style of reporting that bordered on arrogance." Journalists, he concluded, were making decisions for their listeners and readers without knowing enough about them. "News judgments ought to be based on something beyond our seat-of-the-pants notions, or the 'news sense' we're so proud of." The aim of the NPR election project was "to bring citizens back into the center of our coverage," in a departure from the traditional, candidate-centered focus. "What we overlooked was the process that goes on with people as they think and talk and make up their minds. Later I read a lot of books and I realized they call that 'deliberation.'"

Journalists who observe deliberation in action can learn something they might miss from polling data or one-on-one interviews: what happens to people as they encounter the ideas of others who have different experiences but often similar concerns. Dinges adds that NPR reporters also contribute to the discussion by raising difficult questions, injecting facts where they are missing, and correcting misimpressions that have taken hold in the public mind. Thus, emphasizing deliberation does not mean simply handing the microphone over to citizens; rather, it holds citizens to a respectable standard of discourse. It adds a new task to the journalist's job description—the cultivation of "civic" dialogue—to complement the aggressive questioning of public officials. "Some of us are beginning to realize that the democratic process should be more like a town square, where people come to a sense of the public interest, in addition to their own private interest," Dinges observed.

This is hardly a sentiment original to journalists. What is novel is the recognition that the news constitutes a kind of daily advertisement for certain images of political life. "When we treat compromise as a sign of defeat, or when we focus on the extremes to create a 'balanced' story, we're sending a message about politics," Dinges observed. That message needs to change and grow with the times, he believes. "In 1970 and '73 the society needed us to be watchdogs, critical of the system. I was very inspired by that. But today there is something else being asked of us, in addition to the watchdog role: we have to do our job in a way that allows people to do their jobs as citizens."

This is a fine statement of the public journalism creed.

At the *Virginian-Pilot* in Norfolk, the editors have endorsed the change in approach. In April 1995 the *Pilot* inaugurated (on the front page) a new feature called "Democracy and Citizenship: Creating New Conversations." It is intended to stimulate more productive dialogue on controversies in the news. In announcing its plans, the paper told readers,

> More and more Americans hate politics, seeing it mostly as mudslinging and manipulation. Many see government moving further away from citizens. The media often seem to focus on the sensational instead of things that matter in everyday life. The *Virginian-Pilot* would like to play a role in turning around that trend. By rethinking the way we write and report stories, the newspaper hopes to do more than deliver frustrating accounts of problems and mayhem; we want to create a conversation about how to make public life better in Hampton Roads.

An initial effort in this direction examined a bitter debate within the Virginia Republican Party over Senator John Warner's refusal to endorse Oliver North, the party's 1994 nominee for the second Senate seat. Rather than simply report on the backbiting and name-calling that resulted, the *Pilot* tried to engage its readers in dialogue about the serious issues bubbling beneath the surface. The paper asked, "When does party loyalty strengthen political life? When does party loyalty undermine political life?"[7] It then invited responses in a variety of formats; more than three hundred people replied. Most went well beyond the immediate flap (whether Warner was a "creep" or a "hero") to discuss how political conscience could be weighed against the need for strong parties.

After summarizing the themes of the first batch of responses, the *Pilot* asked readers to question themselves. "If you tend to disagree with Warner's actions, in what part of his argument can you find merit? Even if you tend to agree with Warner's actions, what part of his argument do you have problems with? Where is the common ground?"[8] The results of this second round were reported the following week. "This is where we started . . . ," the paper wrote in summarizing the entire discussion. "This is what we learned . . ."[9]

"We're trying to see if our news columns can be used for serious political discussion," explained Dennis Hartig, deputy managing editor of the *Pilot.*[10] "What passes for discussion now tends to be superficial: my opinion, your opinion, agree, disagree. There is no challenge to think and learn from each other, or to see the merit in other points of view." By presenting the new feature on the front page, the *Pilot* was making a statement about its own priorities: serious dialogue is as important as breaking news. According to this philosophy, journalists cannot afford to be neutral on whether public discussion succeeds or falters. "I've seen the gridlock in local communities because they don't know how to have a useful dialogue and make decisions," said Hartig. "One conversation is not going to change journalism or democracy. We know that. But if we can help create the capacity for dialogue through our work, maybe over time that will change politics."

Challenges like "creating capacity" and "changing politics" sound to many of Hartig's colleagues like inappropriate tasks for the press. Understandably leery about aligning themselves with partisan interests, journalists often picture the press as standing outside the political community. Others "do" politics; the press reports on what they do. Among other defects, this view is false with respect to a good deal of journalism's history. One example: When investigative reporting arose at the turn of the century, it was a powerful instrument of the progressive movement, which tried to critique concentrations of power and challenge the grip of the two major parties. The ideology of that era is still dear to many a journalist's heart. "We are progressive reformers, deeply skeptical of all major institutions of society except our own," writes Paul Taylor about himself and his colleagues.[11]

When the *New York Times* created its op-ed page in 1970, it added to the political culture a new and highly visible space, set aside for the daily exchange of ideas. Who is to say that this history cannot have new chapters, that journalism cannot again find dramatic ways of adding to civic capacity and strengthening political culture? The editors of the *Virginian-Pilot* are not about to relinquish that possibility, and this is a large part of what public journalism means to them.

At a retreat I helped organize for the staff of the *Pilot*, fifty reporters and editors spent a weekend struggling with the implications of public journalism for their work. Required readings for the retreat filled a small notebook; they included selections from de Tocqueville's *Democracy in America* and other works of democratic theory and press criticism. Officials of Landmark Communications, which owns the paper, attended as full participants. The entire event was on the record, and a representative from the community who attended later wrote about her impressions, which were carried in the newspaper. This, too, is public journalism: deliberation applied to reform of the press.

At the retreat, editor Cole Campbell gave a talk to his colleagues in which he traced the development of his own philosophy of journalism. He began with an image of the reporter as investigator. "Here the journalist aggressively covers—or uncovers—what happened and tells readers about it." This view treats the rest of the world as the journalist's client, equipped with reliable information and professional advice in order to make intelligent decisions. Campbell later came to appreciate the storytelling model, in which a character faces a troubling predicament and tries to resolve it. This approach sees readers as spectators, "showing them what happened and hoping they will experience an 'aha!'—a moment of revelation" into human nature or present reality.

The third perspective Campbell arrived at he called a "conversational model," his term for public journalism. Here "the journalist works to give readers a way to talk about the news—among family, friends and associates, and among members of the larger community." Readers are regarded not as clients receiving a professional service, or spectators to a compelling public drama but as "people who have a stake in the news, who want to see the possibilities behind often-troubling developments, who want to participate in solving shared problems." Campbell described the fact-finding, storytelling, and conversational models not as warring philosophies but as component parts of a "three-legged stool." As he later wrote: "All three legs are needed to keep superior journalism upright."[12] Campbell ended his talk on a personal note, an effort to explain to his staff where his journey through journalism had led. "My daughter is twenty years old," he said, "and I want her to live in a democracy. Right now I have my doubts."

6/The Journalist as Activist

M ost of the controversy surrounding civic journalism has cen-
tered not on its critique of the "disconnect," its different way of
imagining political life, its embrace of deliberative dialogue, or its concern about the future of democracy, but on a single aspect of some
newspaper experiments: their plunge into what is called "activism" or
"advocacy."

To most of the American press, "advocacy journalism" is an anath-
ema, and so the familiar charge is also a serious one. No movement
could hope to succeed if it tried to persuade journalists to become advocates for a partisan "cause"—especially one they believed in. An acute
wariness of being co-opted is one of the most prominent—and
admirable—features of the professional culture of the press. More than
most outsiders realize, journalists wage a daily struggle to separate
their observations from their personal feelings, and they react with a
certain intensity when they hear it suggested that this struggle is
doomed or can be discarded.

Jane Eisner, editorial page editor of the *Philadelphia Inquirer*,
further explained this attitude in a column on public journalism:

> Corny as it sounds, difficult at it may be to accept, not far
> beneath our cynicism is a great well of idealism and a belief
> that by providing information and nourishing the free flow of
> ideas, we can help make the world a slightly better place.
> Improve those schools, we demand. Fix the health care sys-
> tem. Stop the corrupt politician. And when the stories are
> not enough, we do wonder if there's another step we can
> take.
>
> But many fear that by shedding the cloak of impartiality, by
> becoming participants, we run the great risk of destroying

59

our most precious mandate: to *independently* report, analyze and deliver the news.

"Detached or engaged? Audience or actor?" Eisner asks in her column.[1] This way of putting the question nevertheless obscures what public journalism is really about. It is not a thirst for "engagement" or "action"
that drives its most proactive experiments. It is a growing sense that,
despite a lot of aggressive reporting and angry editorials, often a community's problems continue unresolved—even, at times, undiscussed. In
these circumstances—where "journalism" has effectively ground to a
halt—an editor's choices narrow down to two: Should I remain within
the conventions of the craft and accept the impotence of journalism? Or
should I rethink what "journalism" can be in hopes of stimulating some
kind of discussion and useful engagement? Note that it is the *community's* will to act that is at issue, not the journalist's desire to "advocate."
When articles and editorials are not enough, does the responsibility of
the press extend to other forms of prodding, those for which the newspaper might be well suited? Or should journalists be exempt from any
further duties once they have reported the news and demanded of us,
"Improve those schools. . . . Fix that health care system?"

As Davis Merritt observes, this is really a question of values.
Journalists act on their beliefs all the time, for instance, in their zeal to
investigate a corrupt official. "If we are willing to act on such beliefs as
politicians should not steal, companies should not pollute, and people
should not be exploited, what about other, broader, but similarly fundamental statements: that this should be a better community; that its
problems should be solved; that public life should go well?"[2] Public
journalism suggests harnessing the power of the press toward these
ends, but it does not assume that *journalists* can themselves create a
"better community," solve problems, or "fix" public life through their
own resources. Rather, the emphasis is on supporting the efforts of
citizens, and this is what gets labeled "activism."

To bring the argument into sharper focus, consider the efforts
of the *Herald-Dispatch* in Huntington, West Virginia, an area stricken
by the loss of 70,000 mining and manufacturing jobs over a ten-year
period. In November 1993, the paper, owned by Gannett, published a
twelve-page special section on core weaknesses in the local economy
and choices facing the region if job security, a bedrock concern, was
to be restored. Teaming up with the local NBC affiliate, the paper
then sponsored a public meeting on economic development that
drew more than nine hundred people. Six task forces emerged to
address specific problems, encompassing education and training,

infrastructure needs, industrial development, and other needs. The paper helped recruit citizen volunteers for the task forces and sponsored a follow-up meeting two months later, which drew another 750 people.[3]

As the citizen task forces began to deliberate about steps the community might take to rebuild its economy, the newspaper maintained a supporting role. The *Herald-Dispatch* promised the volunteers that their efforts would not go unnoticed as long as they continued to meet and make progress. In addition to news reports the paper offered them guest columns so that their views could be heard by the larger community. When several groups found they needed more information, particularly about the experience of other cities in rebuilding a job base, the newspaper dispatched reporters to Tupelo, Mississippi, and Russellville, Kentucky, to learn how regions with comparable problems had approached the task. "They presented us with a question, and we answered it—in the paper," said Randy Hammer, editor at the time. "It was our way of maintaining the dialogue."

Often the issue of economic redevelopment is monopolized by powerful business interests and government agencies. But when the daily newspaper gets involved, it can employ its influence to widen the conversation. This was one aim of the *Herald-Dispatch*'s efforts: to create a larger and more inclusive arena for public deliberation on the region's economy. The insiders who customarily dominate such discussions were thus joined by workers, teachers, parents, religious figures, and young people. As the citizen task forces showed more and more promise, the traditional power structure took notice. The economic development committee of the local chamber of commerce actually voted to disband and re-form as a larger, more representative body that included, among others, the trade union head, the school superintendent, the president of the teacher's union, a local rabbi, and a prominent minister.

"They went from fifteen to twenty Chamber types to a far more diverse group of 100 members," Hammer said. "We kept thinking that people would get tired of all the work and all the meetings, but somehow they didn't. And they kept coming to us for help." The paper agreed to broker a meeting between city officials and the citizen task forces that resulted in an application for federal funds under the Clinton administration's community block grant program. In December 1994, Huntington received $3 million from Washington for economic development, later matched by $1 million from the state. Before the task forces began meeting, the city had had no plans to apply for the federal money.

"We brought people into the same room," said Hammer in reflecting on the newspaper's role. "Our goal was to get the community to
come together and address issues it was unable to face before. The
unions and the business people would beat each other up, but they
didn't know how to talk together." Before assuming responsibility as
conveners and brokers of discussion, journalists at the *Herald-
Dispatch* were forced to consider their own contribution to a climate
of mutual mistrust. "What we've traditionally done in journalism is
portray people as stuck in opposite corners," Hammer remarked.
"Here we tried to say there's a middle ground you all share."

Any such effort does create a conflict between the newspaper's
supportive role as a convener of civic dialogue and its more traditional duty to report on what happens in political life. When disputes arose
within the citizen groups, the paper was obligated to report them. But,
as Hammer put it, "we tried not to push people to the edges of the circle." He urged citizens to air their differences in the opinion section of
the *Herald-Dispatch* when they concerned important questions of policy. Finally, he asked an experienced local columnist to write about
the task forces from an outsider's position; he gave the author his personal word that no column would be censored.

Such measures will never satisfy skeptics who reject the convener's role as inappropriate. They would be quick to point out that in
reporting on the task forces, the *Herald-Dispatch* could not feel as
unconstrained as a newspaper with no investment in the process. To
many in the press, such facts seal the indictment against public journalism; it becomes "boosterism" in their minds, an abandonment of
the all-important watchdog role. These critics are defending an
important principle: the press must show courage and independence
in standing up to powerful forces in the community who want to run
things their way. Journalists must be willing to challenge conventional thinking, shake up a complacent community, expose what's
rotten or retrograde in the status quo. They cannot do this if they are
part of the system, and so they need to remain detached from all
"causes," no matter how civic-minded or well-intentioned the cause
seems to be.

Those who have been experimenting with public journalism share
many of these convictions; they were raised on them. None wants to be
part of a tamer press. But they have begun to ask themselves a difficult
question, which remains taboo in most newsrooms: What is the proper distance from which to critique a community? After all, journalists
who are regarded as "messengers from another world," as Howard
Kurtz put it, are hardly in a position to challenge anybody. They are so

detached from the people they may want to confront that no useful confrontation can take place.

This is not a debating point. Consider the troubled relationship between minority populations in big-city neighborhoods and the metropolitan dailies that tend to report on these areas through the lens of crime and social pathology. This pattern enrages local residents, who claim (with considerable justification) that they are being exploited by a news formula that cannot do justice to the realities of their lives. When the newspaper and its reporters are regarded as the "white media"—as they are in many minority neighborhoods—what becomes of their watchdog role? It evaporates.

I have taken a severe example to make a general point: if journalists are to have any sort of critical voice or challenging role within a community, they must live in some fashion as *members* of that community. The force of their reporting will originate not in the distance they keep but in the connection they make to the real aspirations and daily struggles of the people they report to. A certain distance is indeed required, but the distancing can only begin once the connection has been made. If the thread of trust and sympathy is broken, or never established, "tough" reporting falls on indifferent ears. It becomes impotent.

The whole notion of toughness as a property inherent in journalism and journalists is deeply misleading. What makes tough reporting effective as an act of communication is the same thing that makes a trusted friend the best person to give us the painful criticism we sometimes need. Truth-telling at its most difficult draws on the strength of a prior relationship, a bond deep enough to withstand the strain of asserting uncomfortable or depressing facts. So it is in daily journalism. The watchdog must know the house, be minimally welcome in the yard, understand the occupants well enough to sound the right alarm. These are genuine problems of connection. They cannot be waved away with pious rhetoric about "detachment" and scare stories about "getting into bed" with the authorities. Public journalism is not about the authorities. It is about regaining a relationship in which journalists and their publics understand and value each other.

Hodding Carter III, whose family ran a Mississippi newspaper well-known for challenging the community during the civil rights era, had some strong words for those who define civic journalism as an abandonment of the watchdog role: "We debate as though we honestly believe that we can't chew gum and walk down the steps at the same time, that we cannot involve people in the process and at the same time speak truth to power," Carter said. Journalists are "already participants," he added. They are "players" who regard their own "team" as the veritable "fourth branch of government." And they are well-connected to people with power and influence.

> What civic journalism says is let us reconnect with those who are not now on the beat system, who are not already those anointed with power, with standing, with prestige, with an avenue or voice. Civic journalism says let us listen to the people and let us give them voice and let us hear what they have to say about those we routinely cover.

Carter reflected on his family paper's ability to be "involved" in the community while spiking its conscience at the same time, which "brought us the highest penetration of our circulation area of any paper" in Mississippi.

> You can look it up. Because we told that community we cared and we listened to that community while we kicked ass. If you can't do them both, get out of the business.
> We are parts of an organism, we are parts of a process, we are parts of something living, not sterile, not textbook, not detached.[4]

From this perspective an initiative like the *Herald-Dispatch*'s is not about crossing lines separating "journalism" from "advocacy" but *repairing* the lines that connect journalists to a public that would otherwise have no voice in economic planning and chamber of commerce discussions. Aware of the risks involved, the editors and reporters did what they could to anticipate conflicts and avoid damaging compromises. "We had a meeting every day where reporters and editors would talk about the process," Randy Hammer said. "The main concern was always, 'Whose pocket are we in?'"

To their legitimate fears of being co-opted the editors found a disarmingly simple answer: freedom of the press. "We had to control what we wrote," Hammer explained. "As long as everyone understood that, we felt comfortable reporting on the process." Freedom of the press is what Hammer guaranteed to his columnist. The guarantee is only as good as the editor's word, but this is just another way of saying that responsibility in journalism rests on a core of personal integrity.

The Huntington project is the sort of enterprise that raises fears among skeptics like Jane Eisner, who see getting involved as either an abuse of press power or a surrender of independence. The concerns are genuine, and there is no way to "prove" through argument alone that a more proactive press can also be a fair, truthful, and critical voice in the community. That proposition can only be demonstrated—for example, by careful study of the reporting done at the *Herald-Dispatch* during the period of its experiment in community service.

Did the newspaper take unacceptable risks by becoming more proactive? The answer cannot come from journalism and its values alone. The fortunes of the community, the "facts on the ground" as they say in the Middle East, are also relevant in deciding what good journalism is and what chances a responsible editor should take. "Fix the economy," the *Herald-Dispatch* could have roared from the safety of its editorial page. When no one did fix it, the newspaper might have roared some more. The conventions of journalism would have been served. But what about the people of Huntington?

7/The Press Is a Player

It is rarely discussed in newsrooms, but the claim that the press is ordinarily free of involvement in the political process is dubious at best. Any visitor to the country in the grip of such a claim would be helpless to understand the vagaries of American politics. There are dozens of routine ways in which journalists, despite their intention of taking a neutral role, "interfere" in events and influence their outcomes. Here are a few of the more obvious examples.

1. The "invisible primary" early in a presidential campaign in which reporters inform us of the likely front-runners, and thereby cause them to become front-runners by, for instance, lending dramatic support to their fund-raising efforts;

2. Decisions to exclude from news coverage those candidates who, in the reporter's estimation, have no chance of winning, thereby ensuring that their ideas receive scarce hearing and that their campaigns—which may be symbolic in the first place—have a limited effect;

3. "Feeding frenzies" among the press pack that, begun by a hint of scandal, take on a life of their own and through sheer momentum cripple or destroy a candidacy before voters have a chance to evaluate its worth;

4. Political advertisements, usually negative in tone, that air a handful of times as paid announcements and are then replayed many dozens of times as "news," consequently reaching a vastly wider audience and greatly multiplying their effect;

5.   Covert alliances between reporters seeking a front-page story and confidential sources who have an interest in floating a trial balloon or killing a proposed policy through premature publicity;

6.   Investigations of corruption or wrongdoing where the hoped-for effect is legislative action to correct the abuse, resignation of a disgraced public figure, pressure on prosecutors to indict, or some similar result that would win applause and impress the juries that award Pulitzer Prizes.

Examples like these, common as they are, do not illuminate the far larger, if more subtle, influence that journalists exert simply by selecting what makes the front page or leads the evening news, by dropping a story after a few days, or by returning to it again and again. When they permit themselves to reflect on such facts, most journalists understand how they are engaged in shaping the public agenda. They may even aspire to do just that. But they do not define these decisions as "becoming involved" precisely because they are so routine. The "becoming" part isn't visible anymore.

I do not mean to suggest that the journalist's influence on political life is by nature odious, conspiratorial, or corrupt. It is merely routine. Sometimes the press interferes in a way that serves a compelling public purpose; often, it seems arbitrary, thoughtless, or self-serving in the extreme. When Merritt describes the ideal journalist as a "fair-minded participant" in public life,[1] his aim is not to prepare the ground for advocacy journalism but to strike a blow for intellectual honesty. Journalists, he recognizes, are public actors, even though they regularly describe themselves as observers. True, they do not (and should not) "act" in the same way that politicians, lobbyists, bureaucrats, or voters do. But they still act, meaning they exercise their discretion and influence events.

In *The Media and the Mayor's Race*, scholar Phyllis Kaniss tracked the press coverage of Philadelphia's 1991 contest for mayor, interviewing all the major participants, including the candidates and their staffs. She describes how in designing a campaign any competent candidate had to factor in the peculiar obsessions of political journalism. About the thinking of Democrat Ed Rendell, the eventual winner, she writes:

At a journalist's newspaper like the *Inquirer*, political reporting no longer meant reporting what the candidates said about issues of substance. Even though Rendell planned to focus his campaign on the issues, generating position papers on all the city's problems, he knew those positions would not get much ink. Instead, the reporters would analyze why the candidates said what they did. Or worse, they would not even report what the candidates said, at least not in any comprehensive way, but rather would pick out an isolated sentence here and there with which to stir up controversy where none existed, to make the election more interesting.[2]

Rendell knew he could be hurt by two predictable themes. One was the charge that he "couldn't get the black vote" as a white competing against black Democrats in the primary. The other was the appeal of the "outsider," in this case a prominent attorney named Peter Hearn who had never run for office. Both would count as "interesting" to reporters who were only interested in only certain things. Kaniss continues:

> . . . there was only one way that Rendell [and his advisors] could counteract this. They would appeal to the media's preoccupation with the horse race and reporters' unquestioning reverence for numbers. They would use polls. Reporters don't want your housing program, Rendell would say, but they love to talk about polls. And so Rendell and his media strategists determined at the outset of the campaign to use polls to their advantage. They would try to make it seem that Peter Hearn was a total longshot, that nobody thought he was a credible candidate, and that he wasn't making any headway with the public. And they would use polls to show that Rendell would get a sizable chunk of the black vote. . . . [They understood] that being the best known—and generally liked—meant that you could dominate the polls early on. And they knew that those polls would be picked up by all the political reporters in town. . . .[3]

That politicians try to work the press to their advantage is hardly news. Nor is it a scandal that it sometimes works. What Kaniss shows in disturbing detail is that the weaknesses of political journalism—its obsession with polls, strategy, winning and losing—have transmuted into weaknesses in public dialogue, as candidates and advisers react to what they know journalists will do. Everyone involved understands the press as a player; any candidate (or reporter) who overlooked this would be at a major disadvantage. Again, there is no scandal there.

What is troublesome is the *quality of play* the press encourages by its own behavior—its relentless insider mentality, its hunger for cheap drama, its obsession with winning.

By now the rituals and rewards attached to political journalism have made it an obstacle to serious public discourse. Economic pressures and staff reductions in the newsroom, along with the unraveling of the American metropolis, are a big part of the explanation, as Kaniss shows. Equally relevant, however, is the journalist's lens on the political scene, the definition of what counts as news. The proposition that "voters are entitled to have the candidates talk about the issues in depth," so central to the early experiments in Wichita and Charlotte, was *not* central in the Philadelphia mayor's race because journalists, who are key players in the campaign, did not make it so.

Professional lore in journalism still contends, against every sort of evidence, that the press is a bystander, a political innocent, uninvolved in the events under its scrutiny. That is why Dave Tucker, city editor of the *Inquirer*, can separate himself from public journalism by saying, "This stuff about becoming a part of the story and the reporting about yourself is . . . for the birds."[4] Of course, that is exactly what the *Inquirer* did in 1991: it reported on a Rendell campaign that was shaped early on by the paper's own obsession with polling numbers. The *Inquirer* and its predictable routines were "part of the story" before the story even unfolded. But were they a useful part? Did they serve a compelling public purpose?

Public journalism is controversial, I believe, not because it demands that journalists get involved, but because it lifts their involvement into public view, acknowledging what everyone already knows: the press is a player. It then proceeds to ask: *For what and for whom should the press be playing?* The answers offered are certain public values: civic participation, deliberative dialogue, politics as problem solving, and the cultivation of "democratic dispositions."

A public climate that earns our respect because it addresses our concerns, welcomes our involvement, and demands from us our most mature selves—in general, this is what public journalists are willing to be "for." How to translate such values into journalism that is aggressive and alive is the practical problem the movement is trying to solve. No one pretends that the answer has been found, which is why the approach is still experimental. What seemed to work in Charlotte would be unworkable in Philadelphia, what the community might welcome in Huntington would be absurdly out of place in New York. But the priorities of civil dialogue, public participation and politics as problem-solving apply everywhere. "Democratic dispositions" are everywhere in need.

Any editor who goes looking for opportunities to "get involved" misunderstands the message of the movement—"to do our job in a way that allows people to do their jobs as citizens," as John Dinges put it. Neutrality is not abandoned in this approach but relocated, for there are many ways to find a neutral position in the drama of public life. One is the neutrality of the observer high up in the press box; but there is also the neutrality of the referee keeping things in order on the field of play. There is the neutrality of the critic or "analyst," judging the action from a distance; but there is also the neutrality of the catalyst, persuading people to engage each other, then stepping back. The reporter's role is a neutral one; but so is the convener's. Those involved in public journalism are not making political alliances, pursuing ideological causes, carrying out their private agendas, or tossing aside the virtues of an independent press. They merely wish to experiment with different styles of neutrality, searching for the best way to address the disconnect.

Is public journalism a marketing gimmick, as some in the press have charged? Done in a superficial and cynical way, it could easily become one. A profit-hungry news executive looking for a new promotional ploy can abuse almost any approach, and there is plenty of rich material in the rhetoric of public journalism. What is really at issue here is: Who shall determine the response to the widely noted disconnect? Public journalism suggests that journalists come forward with an intelligent and aggressive program of their own, or watch the marketeers take over. There is a huge difference, however, between the thrust of product marketing—"figure out what they want and give it to them"—and what public journalism says: "uncover what concerns people in their role as citizens, and work to make politics and journalism address those troubles." Those inclined to erase this difference are doing their colleagues in civic journalism an injustice.

In cataloguing familiar criticisms of the movement, I have found one prominent feature of public journalism that goes virtually unmentioned: the willingness to discuss publicly the assumptions and aspirations that shape news coverage. When Dennis Hartig of the *Virginian-Pilot* went before the local League of Women Voters to explain public journalism, he emphasized that the paper wanted to address people as problem-solvers and to frame public issues as potentially solvable. The League decided to take him up on it. It conducted an audit of the paper's coverage for a month, then sent the results to the *Pilot* with detailed criticisms of where the editors had met their goal and where they had fallen short. As the report stated, "The *Virginian-Pilot*'s commitment to this approach must be evaluated before it may be declared a success; citizens must examine its implementation and outcomes." The *Pilot* printed the results of the audit in its Sunday edition and said to League: keep it up.[5]

If silence about the values behind its own agenda is one factor in mistrust of the press (I believe it is), public journalism should then be seen as an effort to make news organizations more accountable to the public they serve. By explaining in print the priorities that will drive their coverage, and by asking for the participation of citizens in shaping a news agenda and evaluating the results, the editors involved are experimenting with the sort of open dialogue the press needs to have with its many angry and alienated constituencies.

Those in the profession who are unwilling to be held accountable (or share power) in a similar fashion might want to explain to those who *are* willing why such practices are foolhardy or unneeded. I would like to hear them try. They are likely to discover an unpublicized fact: the frontier in press accountability is crowded with public journalists who are taking the risks that come with being candid about matters traditionally cloaked in professional mystique.

8/A CHALLENGE TO THE NATIONAL PRESS

Osborn Elliott, the former editor of *Newsweek* and ex-dean of Columbia University's journalism school, has grown impatient with his former colleagues and the "chilly remove" at which they conveniently place themselves. In a 1995 lecture Elliott said it was "Time, I think, for us journalists to change our ways—not by becoming advocates for particular policies but by helping the public gain confidence in its own ability to reach consensus and solve problems. It's time for journalism to abandon cynicism, to uncurl its lip and to become a fair-minded participant and catalyst in America's decision-making process."[1]

David Broder of the *Washington Post* said much the same thing five years earlier. "It is time for those of us in the world's freest press to become activists, not on behalf of a particular party or politician, but on behalf of the process of self-government," he wrote. "We have to help reconnect politics and government—what happens in the campaign and what happens afterward in public policy."[2] It turned out that there was a constituency for Broder's declaration, but it was not his colleagues in the national press corps. Rather, his call for a more "activist" press helped inspire some of the early experiments in public journalism at the local level. These put into practice his intelligent distinction between partisan advocate and civic catalyst.

In contrast to Broder's message—that the press will have to become more active in defense of democratic values—stands the attitude of Max Frankel: "Reporters, editors and publishers have their hands full learning to tell it right. They should leave reforms to the reformers." Which of these views triumphs in the mind of the American press will be a cultural drama worth watching in the years ahead, as important to the *New York Times* as it is to the *Wichita Eagle*.

There are heavyweights on both sides. But the outcome is certain to be shaped by how journalists see themselves in relation to the political community on the one hand and the media industry on the other.

Journalists persuaded of the deeper implications of what Robert MacNeil was saying ("We have to remember . . . that we may be observers but we are not totally disinterested observers") will be more likely to place themselves inside the polity and accept some responsibility for democracy's repair and revival, even if that means questioning familiar conventions. Others will continue to stand outside, leaving reforms to the reformers, in the belief that better execution of the existing model will prove adequate, perhaps with some creative adjustments for new technologies. It is interesting to note that Max Frankel is far more optimistic than MacNeil about the prospects for journalism in the coming media environment:

> . . . the better newspapers ought to feel at home in the next century. They are, by definition, "interactive"—providing well-stocked shelves of news and ads that an educated person might want to read and yet requiring the consumer to navigate the aisles of this supermarket. The choices in cyberspace will be vastly greater, of course; the consumer will find it easy to wander through many markets. The meaty political news may come from one store; the investment proteins from another; the gossipy desserts from yet another. But all the goods will have been selected and displayed by someone somehow—"served" in cyberlingo. Smart journalists and publishers will gradually discover ways to be paid for the serving. Theirs will be the brand names on which the consumer grows to depend.[3]

This is a vision of journalism as consumer good, in which news organizations survive as trusty brand names. But will consumers in cyberspace find a way to join in the American experiment as citizens? Surely the "better newspapers" should feel some stake in this question.

Frankel, I trust, wants the journalism of the future to nourish and support democracy, but in his view authoritative information is all that can be expected of the press. He criticizes civic journalists because they are "not content to tell it like it is. They want to tell it and fix it all at once."[4] Two points are missed: first, the challenge of telling the story in a way that helps *communities* (not journalists) do the fixing; and second, the argument, central to public journalism, that facts made public do not a public make. As Davis Merritt puts it:

Traditional journalism insists that it is honest, intelligent, aware, reliable and trustworthy—but insists that it has no broad view of its purpose in life other than to accumulate facts that are relayed as news.

But in a world awash in facts and events, people pay us not merely for information, but our opinion about the relative importance of things. They will trust us in this endeavor and attend to our opinions only if they believe our opinions are based on some broad, shared values.

Public journalism is openly based on such values as: This should be a better place to live, and people should determine what that means by taking personal responsibility for what goes on around them. Public life, according to the values of public journalism, requires shared information and shared deliberation; [with these] people participate in answering democracy's fundamental question of "What shall we do?"[5]

Are the values Merritt invokes here appropriate only to local communities the size of Madison or Wichita? I do not think so. National journalism, caught up in the pathologies of our politics, needs a firmer grounding in the conviction that public life should be a "better place" for citizens to dwell. In this regard, journalists ought to ponder whether cynicism as a professional reflex could be better controlled.

Jonathan Alter, a columnist for *Newsweek*, laid down a provocative challenge along these lines when he took note of press reactions to Newt Gingrich's first trip to the White House as House speaker. Gingrich emerged from the meeting to say he had found substantial common ground with Clinton, an announcement met with unruly disbelief. Gingrich exploded at the press, and his reaction of course made news. Did the speaker have a point? Yet another story about the acrimony in Washington "wouldn't really be news," Alter wrote. "It would be 'olds,' wouldn't it?" As he added in an interview with the *Boston Globe*, "We have to look at assumptions about how we define news. . . . Something falling apart, something failing, something going wrong, that's old. That's not news."[6]

Alter seems to be searching for an alternative to a "disease" model of political life, in which things become interesting only when they begin to break down. The 1996 campaign is a perfect opportunity to experiment with styles of journalism that transcend pathology and reach beyond the demystification of politics to its repair and revival. Will the press respond in a spirit of experimentation? Or will it settle for half-measures and marginal improvements?

A bold example has already been set by Tom Hamburger, Washington bureau chief of the *Star Tribune* in Minneapolis. He calls it the "Minnesota Compact," a proposal floated with the aim of improving public dialogue during the 1996 Senate race in his state. The compact— presented as Hamburger's idea, not *Star Tribune* policy— reckons with all the familiar frustrations with electoral politics: the lack of thoughtful discussion, the attack ads that do so much to heighten public cynicism, press coverage that fails to confront people's central concerns, and citizens who turn away in boredom or revulsion.

Hamburger became alarmed when the 1994 elections brought to Minnesota the same negative ads that were eviscerating campaign dialogue elsewhere in the country. He noted, as well, that 1994 brought a record low voter turnout for a midterm election. Blessed with a strong civic culture, Minnesotans had come to expect a more reasoned tone to prevail in their politics. As Hamburger discussed the drift of affairs with people active in both parties, he found a near unanimous sense that the new rules ("destroy your opponent and do it early") were regrettable and foreign to the state's public spirit. "It was clear that '96 would be a disaster if there wasn't some intervention," Hamburger told me in an interview. "Everyone I talked to expressed a desire to end the cycle. But they also felt locked into a system that went against their better judgment."[7]

The Minnesota Compact is designed to break the pattern and make it possible for the state's "better judgment" to win out. The proposal has four parts:

1. Eight debates or "community discussions" would be organized by a private sponsor during the 1996 Senate race, one in each congressional district, some on single topics like welfare or education. Press conferences after the event would allow for follow-up questions. Only the candidates who agreed to the compact would be invited to participate.

2. "Candidates must face the camera for the duration of any paid political advertising submitted for television broadcast. There is no restriction on what the candidate might say. But the use of prepared film footage—whether dramatizing the threat of a released convict or a candidate's face morphing into that of an unpopular figure—would be prohibited. Candidates who breach this plank of the compact would be ineligible to participate in the debates."

3. "News organizations would emphasize the substantive concerns of citizens, addressing competing proposals for dealing with those

concerns with the gusto we reserve for coverage of the O.J. Simpson trial or the Super Bowl." Journalists would agree to "cover the debates and follow-up press conferences, emphasize substance over style in campaigns, and provide in-depth coverage of community concerns." Editors would be held "responsible for making measurable changes."

4.   "[We] Minnesota citizens commit ourselves to participating, setting clearer and higher standards for political discourse among candidates and citizens. Citizens will designate an hour before the first fall debate to consider what's at stake in the election. And for one hour on each of the subsequent debate days, families and churches and labor groups and private clubs will gather together, participating in a statewide discussion. We're accustomed to hosting gatherings like this for the Super Bowl. We'll use the debates as an opportunity . . . to talk about common concerns—and to demand restoration of rational thinking and discussion in our political contests."[8]

Hamburger's hope is that broad public collaboration in an alternative system of discourse might prevail over the destructive cycle of attack ads and the sound-bite politics they support. Candidates, civic groups, citizens, and journalists must all do their part.

Aware of the ferment surrounding public journalism, Hamburger had come to believe that he and his colleagues were not exempt from acting against the decline of rational discourse and its predictable result: deeper cynicism. "One thing we should be willing to stand for as journalists is high quality public dialogue," he maintained. "Not only should we call for quality, we can go on to advocate it and suggest ways to bring it about. And it's in our interest to do so." Hamburger called newspapers "one of the last common denominators in American society," well-suited to be a caretaker of civic discussion. "We have a role in helping the community identify its concerns and get them resolved," he said. "If the system gets off track, if we aren't really talking about common problems, then it's our responsibility to call the debate back, and keep the discussion focused."

By speaking in the "we" voice, the Minnesota Compact incorporates the press into the political community, giving it a duty to support civic traditions now threatened with eclipse. It also challenges the fiction of the journalist as someone without a political life, for in trying to rescue Minnesota from a fate that has befallen other polities, Hamburger was clearly standing up for a certain kind of politics—

grounded in oratory, rational argument, civility, and public deliberation—against the "attack" style, which is image-based and ruled by
an ethic of destruction. When it was suggested to Hamburger that his
proposal would give an advantage to candidates who were skilled public speakers, he agreed. "That's one of the biases."[8]

Unwilling to "leave reforms to the reformers," but wary about pro-
ceeding alone, Hamburger chose to draw on America's oldest political
tradition, the notion of a compact, mutually binding on all who join it.
Far from destroying the independence or freedom of the press, the
compact actually honors those principles, for only those who are free
and independent can agree to be mutually bound. By acknowledging
their duty to "emphasize substance over style in campaigns, and provide in-depth coverage of community concerns," news organizations
make public use of their freedom and link their First Amendment guar-
antees to important principles of accountability. They declare what
they are willing to be "for." The entire proposal should be seen as
strengthening press freedom because it illustrates to all why we have a
free press: so that our common affairs may be conducted well.

In the spring of 1995 a consortium of news organizations in New
Hampshire—including New Hampshire Public Television, New
Hampshire Public Radio, a commercial television station, two newspapers, and later the New Hampshire Associated Press—set forth a
mission statement describing its aims for campaign coverage in 1996.
Here are some of the rules by which the New Hampshire consortium
agrees to be bound:

> "Voters' Voice" is a partnership dedicated to making voters'
> issues and voters themselves the focus of news coverage of
> New Hampshire elections in 1996. Its goals include re-estab-
> lishing the role of the electorate by putting their issues first;
> reducing coverage of "campaign issues" that will disappear
> after the election; reducing coverage of mudslinging and
> attacks; promoting fairness and accuracy in campaigns;
> reducing coverage of campaign strategy, personnel changes
> and other insider information; playing down "horse race"
> polling and playing up polling about what voters think and
> how they react to candidates' stands on issues; using news
> coverage to show voters they and their opinions count; and
> using news coverage to emphasize the connection between
> campaigns and governing. Membership in the partnership
> will not inhibit or preclude independent coverage of any can-
> didate or issue by any member.[10]

This statement can be seen as a public challenge to others in the press to meet the standards of disclosure set by their colleagues in New Hampshire.

And what say the editors and reporters at *Time* and *Newsweek*, the *Washington Post* and the *New York Times*, the *Philadelphia Inquirer* and the *St. Louis Post Dispatch*? How far are they willing to go in disclosing and defending their own agenda and the assumptions behind it? How many others in journalism will come forward with proposals as daring and public-spirited as Tom Hamburger's? How many are willing to back away from the "Crossfire mentality" that led Teresa Hanafin of the *Boston Globe* in the direction of public journalism?

One of the difficulties of proclaiming a "movement" is that journalists are not joiners by nature, although they are aggressive imitators. Most in the press will probably never call themselves public journalists or embrace the philosophy in any explicit way. If it is going to succeed, public journalism will have to lose its name by dissolving into daily practice. It will then become what some already tell me it is: "just good journalism." What ultimately matters, then, is not how many people sign on and declare themselves believers. What matters is that more and more journalists acknowledge their complicity in a system that is failing citizens and try their best to experiment with thoughtful alternatives, grounded in the conviction that public life can be improved. The 1996 campaign will be interesting to watch for this among other dramas.[11]

9/GETTING THE CONNECTIONS RIGHT

To understand why more journalists aren't willing to act in the spirit of Davis Merritt's philosophy, Tom Hamburger's proposal, and the New Hampshire partnership's mission statement, it is necessary to realize the depths to which the principle of detachment can be taken. Journalists sometimes appear to detach themselves not only from the events they report upon but from the republic they are reporting to. David Broder reflected on this in a 1991 speech. Sounding none too proud of the fact, he noted that "a very large percentage of the information that the American people get about politics comes from people who disclaim any responsibility for the consequences of our politics." The people he referred to were journalists on the one hand and political consultants on the other.[1]

Left unchallenged, a philosophy like "we let the chips fall where they may" can persuade journalists that their duty to truth-telling leaves them no choice but to extinguish their identity as citizens. I once asked a former *New York Times* reporter why he left the paper near the peak of his career. He said he found it intolerable that the institutional culture of the *Times* would not permit him to care about what happens in education, his beat for a time. In upholding what they take to be their professional responsibility, journalists often reach this extreme point of isolation, where they have effectively removed themselves from the political community, whose fortunes remain their quarry but not their concern.

I first reflected on this possibility during the 1992 campaign, when I came across a column written by Broder's editor, Leonard Downie. Downie wanted to explain to *Washington Post* readers that the paper's recent endorsement of Bill Clinton would have no effect on its coverage of the campaign. The "opinion-making and news coverage functions of the paper are kept completely separate," he said. He recognized that journalists are people who "cannot be expected to cleanse their professional minds of human emotions and opinions." And yet, he added, the *Post* wanted its reporters and editors "to come as close as possible to doing just that." He went on: "In the most extreme effort of this kind, *I no longer exercise my right to vote.*"[2]

Personally, I want my newspaper editor to vote, for that is one way he can keep in touch with the beauty and mystery of democracy. But Downie has another concern: he wants his mind to remain as open as possible, and he worries that the act of voting will carry with it a subtle bias toward one candidate or another. Aware of the power he holds as the final judge of editorial policy, he decides to impose on himself a genuine sacrifice: the loss of his vote, a suspension of his own citizenship. He admits that his choice is "extreme," and not likely to appeal to others at the *Post*. All this shows that Downie is a thoughtful and principled man, but the principle is important to examine.

Note first that his sacrifice is unrequested. I know of no press critic, no professional code, no responsible body that has ever asked journalists to relinquish their vote—although everyone expects that the press will be fair and impartial. So it is not only Downie's decision but his manner of deciding that is radically "detached." Second, Downie assumes that the quality of his "news judgment," an editor's stock-in-trade, improves with his distance from the political community. Getting the distance right is his primary concern, and he is willing to take a drastic step to remain properly detached.

Not many journalists go to those lengths, but journalism in general shares Downie's approach. It aims to remain properly detached. The industry's ethical codes are concerned almost exclusively with *getting the separations right*. Consider how central the image of separation is in the mind of the American press:

▲   Editorial functions are separated from the business side.

▲   The news pages are separated from the opinion pages.

▲   Facts are separated from values.

▲   Those who make the news are separated from those who cover the news.

▲   Truth-telling must be separated from its consequences so that journalists can "tell it like it is."

▲   The newspaper is separated from other institutions by its duty to report on them.

▲   One day is separated from another because news is what's "new" today.

▲   A good journalist separates reality from rhetoric.

▲   One's professional identity must be separated from one's personal identity as a citizen.

▲   How one "feels" about something is separate from how one reports on it.

▲   The journalist's mind is separate from the journalist's soul.

But suppose that getting the separations right isn't the central problem. This is what public journalism is saying: *getting the connections right* is the deeper challenge in journalism right now. "Getting the connections right" means all the connections: between news and opinion, between facts and values, between the editorial product and the business function, between the press and the political system, between the occupational and the spiritual crisis, and particularly between journalism and the public. Worry about the connections, and in time the needed separations will become clear. This is a difficult task, primarily because some distancing remains critically important. There is, finally, a difference between doing journalism and doing politics, between observation and action. There is a core value in "objectivity" that ought to be upheld, but, as Ed Fouhy observes, there is also "a sterile detachment from the life of the community" that needs to be overcome.[3]

Of course, journalists must worry about undue bias and conflicts of interest, but they can approach these concerns from another angle. In trying to connect community and polity, they can discover in practice where the important lines need to be drawn. In claiming their place inside the political community, they can learn to detach themselves from the story without removing themselves from the ranks of their fellow citizens, without pretending, as Robert MacNeil put it, that they are "amused bystanders, watching the idiots screw it up."

People in the press need some sense of what they are working toward, what it all adds up to. This sense, earlier characterized as "spiritual," cannot be found within journalism itself. The mission of good journalism is not, I think, to do good journalism. It must be something larger. By tradition, journalism aims to inform the public and act as a watchdog over government. Public journalists regard these things as critically important. But with American democracy in the midst of a deepening ordeal, the times demand something further: By framing the story of politics as *our* story, incomplete without public involvement, journalists can begin recalling us to the civic spirit in which the country was founded.

As James Carey writes, the discussion on which a living democracy depends is "ours to conduct with one another." To Americans themselves goes the task of creating a public realm where the discussion we need can shape the politics we get. "If the established press wants to aid this process, so much the better," Carey observes. But if, bound to routines that serve its own interests, "the press decides to sit out public life, we shall simply have to create a space for citizens and patriots by ourselves."[4]

With or without the help of a civic-minded press, Americans are likely to find new ways of conversing together and solving their problems. Those who entered journalism to make a difference—and there are many—might now begin to ask themselves where the real difference can be made. A skeptical press, telling of our fools and faults, is as necessary as ever. But as citizens we require more than an expert crap detector. We need to find our own entry points into the American story, the places where we can insert ourselves and somehow begin to act. Journalism, if it chooses, can guide us toward these points. If it declines the challenge, other sources of help can and eventually will be found.

10/CONCLUSION

In *Democracy on Trial*, Jean Bethke Elshtain takes note of a "deepening emptiness, a kind of evacuation of civic spaces" that "lies in the background of our current discontents."[1]

Journalists, I have tried to argue, are implicated in this emptiness. Yet, the easiest course for them to follow is to do nothing while their grumbling grows louder and ruder. The next-easiest solution is to address the civic crisis as if it were a commercial problem. In the years ahead, journalists will face increasing pressure from the media to adopt the industry's all-purpose ethic: audience production at the lowest possible cost. But there needs to be a third alternative, beyond the nostalgia for a lost environment and the helpless surrender to a new and far meaner one.

Many people of goodwill are trying to find this third path. No one knows where it lies, and that includes those associated with public journalism. My guess is that the answer involves a different story about democracy and the press, about journalists and citizens, about information and participation. At the risk of exaggerating the difference, I will try to summarize what this "new" story is saying. Two overlapping propositions capture the essence of it:

1. It is commonly assumed that people need to be informed so they can participate. Public journalism proposes the reverse: People have to participate, so that they'll want and need to become informed.

2. Traditional thinking in the press assumes that democracy is what we have and information is what we need. Public journalism says: reverse the proposition and you'll be closer to the truth. Information is what we have—in the media age, information is everywhere—and democracy is what we need.

83

Both propositions assume that citizenship sustains the press. It may be, as some will argue, that our inclination to be citizens, to assume the joys and duties of public life, is a thin reed on which to build a secure and independent press. Ultimately the question of demand has to be faced, and if, in the age of multimedia, there truly is no demand for the journalist's best efforts then the press as an institution is doomed. But no one can say this point has been reached, and it would hardly be in the American spirit to throw up one's hands and accept the demise of an important public art.

Through the machinery of journalism passes the story of our common life. It is the quality of this story that is at stake in journalists' struggle with the media and an angry public. Can the story be effectively told without the press as a reporter, narrator, and intermediary? Perhaps, and there are new possibilities for "unfiltered" news that might be pursued here. But it seems equally likely that the version of the American story most people get will simply deteriorate as it becomes not less filtered but more and more a "media" production— an entertainment like everything else.

This is a challenge to American culture, not just the culture of the press. For those concerned about the drift of politics and public dialogue in recent years, for those with a feel for what Elshtain calls "democratic dispositions," for those who look warily on the hyper-commercialization of our culture, for those concerned about the health of their local communities, now is a good time to join in the discussion of what journalism is—and might yet become. In this sense public journalism needs to involve the public as much as the press.

"We are contemporaries only so far as our understanding reaches," writes another political philosopher, Hannah Arendt.[2] I have often struggled with this provocative thought in trying to grasp precisely why journalism matters. The media, after all, can be counted on to flood us with "information." But Arendt's thought is a reminder that democracy depends on something deeper. Not only must information flow freely, but understanding must range widely: into pockets of misery, halls of power, problems under the surface, opportunities over the horizon, lives unlike our own. Only through discussion, imagination, and serious attention do we begin to live as citizens of the same country, alert to common dangers, alive to common hopes. Arendt's warning is that we can lose our sense of living in the same world with others if some basic understanding of that world is not shared across a multitude of boundaries and divisions. Should the prospect of such a loss seem remote, or the concept abstract, there are the dark headlines from 1995, from Oklahoma City and the militia movement, and from the aftermath of the O. J. Simpson trial, to remind us that the danger is real.

So if journalists furnish us with facts, that is not really the heart of what they do. Even more important than the facts they supply is a political fact they strive to create: the establishment of a shared present, a world of genuinely public concerns, the reality of which is not in doubt, toward which we can take our separate and often conflicting views. This simultaneity of experience, where what is happening "out there" in the public world happens along with the rest of us, is the most valuable thing journalists have to offer. It matters to everyone in a democratic society because it is part of what it means to be a member of that society.

Thus, when journalists lose contact with a majority of the population, when they and the news suffer a decline in public trust, the common world becomes a little less common. At the end of this road is a prospect we do not want to face: divisions far deeper than interest or ideology, grounded in irreconcilable views of what counts as "real." The militia members and black nationalists are already there, holed up in their own world of current events. If there's one thing we know about them, it's that they read the papers with a savage mistrust.

All this need not concern the media industry, which produces its own reality and is rapidly growing beyond the control of any identifiable group or the interest of any national community. Journalists are valuable because they address political publics, which can only be located in the political arena. The media serves markets, which are found everywhere and anywhere. "Anywhere" is exactly where the media tend to place us, for it is the largest market imaginable. *Here*, in this town, this country, at this turn in our collective story, is where journalism at its best positions us.

That position is too valuable to relinquish without a fight.

NOTES

INTRODUCTION

1. See, for example, Ellen Hume, "Tabloids, Talk Radio and the Future of News: Technology's Impact on Journalism," The Annenberg Washington Program, Washington, D.C., 1995, p. 13: "This is a moment of truth for the major news organizations"; Thomas Winship, former editor of the *Boston Globe*, quoted in *Civic Catalyst*, Pew Center for Civic Journalism, Washington, D.C., October 1995, p. 6: "This is a watershed time for the [news] media, to say nothing for the spirit of the country"; Howard Kurtz, *Media Circus: The Trouble with America's Newspapers* (New York: Times Books, 1993), p. 373: "The press is in deep, deep trouble."

2. Carey's remarks are from the transcript of the Project on Public Life and the Press summer seminar at American Press Institute, Reston, Va., August 12–15, 1995, p. 5, available from the Kettering Foundation, Dayton. See also James W. Carey, "The Press, Public Opinion and Public Discourse," in Theodore L. Glasser and Charles T. Salmon, eds., *Public Opinion and the Communication of Consent* (New York: Guilford Press, 1995), pp. 373–402.

3. Robert MacNeil, "Regaining Dignity," *Media Studies Journal* 9, no. 3 (Summer 1995): 110–11.

4. On public or civic journalism generally, see John Bare, "Case Study—Wichita and Charlotte: The Leap of a Passive Press to Activism," *Media Studies Journal* 6, no. 4 (Fall 1992): 149–60; Jay Rosen, *Community-Connectedness: Passwords for Public Journalism*, Poynter Institute for Media Studies, St. Petersburg, Fla., 1993; Jay Rosen and Davis Merritt, *Public Journalism: Theory and Practice* (Dayton: Kettering Foundation, 1994); Davis Merritt, "Public Journalism—Defining a Democratic Art," *Media Studies Journal* 9, no. 3 (Summer 1995): 125–32; Davis Merritt, Jr., *Public Journalism and Public Life: Why Telling the News Is Not Enough* (Hillsdale, N.J.: Lawrence Erlbaum Associates, 1995); Arthur Charity, *Doing Public Journalism* (New York: Guilford Press, 1995); Michael Hoyt, "Are You Now, or Will You Ever Be, a Civic Journalist?" *Columbia Journalism Review*, September/October 1995, pp. 27–33. For specific cases see *Civic Journalism: Six Case Studies*, Pew Center for Civic Journalism, Washington, D.C., 1995. For a discussion of effects see Frank Denton and Esther Thorson, *Civic Journalism: Does it Work?*, Pew Center for

Civic Journalism, Washington, D.C., 1995. For a scholarly account of the idea's origins, see Jay Rosen, "Making Things More Public: On the Political Responsibility of the Media Intellectual," *Critical Studies in Mass Communication* 11, no. 4 (December 1994): 363–88.

5. Bradley's remarks are from the transcript of an August 17, 1995, press conference in Newark, p. 1, available through Federal News Service, Washington, D.C.

6. E. J. Dionne, *Why Americans Hate Politics* (New York: Simon and Schuster, 1991).

7. The Harwood Group, *Citizens and Politics: A View from Main Street America* (Dayton: Kettering Foundation, 1991), p. v.

8. Robert D. Putnam, "Bowling Alone: America's Declining Social Capital," *Journal of Democracy* 6, no. 1 (January 1995): 65–78. See also Robert D. Putnam, "The Prosperous Community: Social Capital and Public Life," *American Prospect*, Spring 1993, pp. 35–42.

9. See Timothy Egan, "Many Seek Security in Private Communities," *New York Times*, September 3, 1995, section I, pp. 1, 22.

10. Jean Bethke Elshtain, *Democracy on Trial* (New York: Basic Books, 1995), p. 5. On the general point, see her first chapter, "Democracy's Precarious Present."

11. See Carl Sessions Stepp, "The Thrill Is Gone," *American Journalism Review*, October 1995, pp. 15–19.

12. For an important critique along these lines, see Thomas E. Patterson, *Out of Order* (New York: Knopf, 1993).

13. On American professionals generally and their need to find a more "civic" identity, see William M. Sullivan, *Work and Integrity: The Crisis and Promise of Professionalism in America* (New York: HarperCollins, 1995).

14. Michael Sandel, *Liberalism and the Limits of Justice* (New York: Cambridge University Press, 1982), p. 183.

CHAPTER 1

1. Quoted in "Talking about the Media Circus," *New York Times Magazine*, June 28, 1994, p. 53.

2. "The New Political Landscape," report of the Times Mirror Center for the People and the Press, Washington, D.C., October 1994, p. 160.

3. Hanafin's remarks are from the transcript of the Project on Public Life and the Press spring seminar at American Press Institute, Reston, Va., March 23–25, 1995, p. 285, available from Kettering Foundation, Dayton.

4. Doug Clifton, executive editor of the *Miami Herald*, writes, "For all our much talked about liberality and tolerance of social change, most journalists are deeply conservative when it comes to their own craft." See Doug Clifton, "Creating a Forum to Help Solve Community Problems," *Miami Herald*, March 6, 1994, p. 4C.

5. Michael Schudson, *Discovering the News: A Social History of American Newspapers* (New York: Basic Books, 1978), p. 9.

6. As press scholars Clifford Christians, John P. Ferre, and P. Mark Fackler observe, "Whenever challenged, the press thrusts the First Amendment forward as a fetish to ward off the spirits of responsibility." See Clifford Christians, John P. Ferre, and P. Mark Fackler, *Good News: Social Ethics and the Press* (New York: Oxford University Press, 1993), p. 53.

7. Linsky adds, "Most journalists interpret the First Amendment as freeing them from [a duty to society] in the ethical and community as well as the legal and constitutional senses." See Martin Linsky, "The Media and Public Deliberation," in Robert B. Reich, ed., *The Power of Public Ideas* (Cambridge, Mass.: Harvard University Press, 1988), p. 211.

8. Michael Janeway, "The Press and Privacy: Rights and Rules," in W. Lawson Taitte, ed., *The Morality of the Mass Media* (Dallas: University of Texas Press, 1994), pp. 129–30.

9. Howard Kurtz, *Media Circus: The Trouble with America's Newspapers* (New York: Times Books, 1993), pp. 6–7. On the same general themes, see Mark Jurkowitz, "Reforming the Media," *Boston Globe Magazine*, July 9, 1995, pp. 18, 20, 22–25, 30–31.

10. Davis Merritt, Jr., *Public Journalism and Public Life: Why Telling the News Is Not Enough* (Hillsdale, N.J.: Lawrence Erlbaum Associates, 1995), p. 10.

CHAPTER 2

1. On the responses to public journalism from journalists see Alicia C. Shepard, "The Gospel of Public Journalism," *American Journalism Review*, September 1994, pp. 28–34; William Glaberson, "A New Press Role: Solving Problems," *New York Times*, October 3, 1994, p. D6; Tony Case, "Public Journalism Denounced," *Editor and Publisher*, November 12, 1994, pp. 14–15; Judith Shepard, "Climbing Down from the Ivory Tower," *American Journalism Review*, May 1995, pp. 18–25; M. L. Stein, "Beware of Public Journalism," *Editor and Publisher*, May 6, 1995, p. 18. A typical critique is Jonathan Cohn, "Should Journalists Do Community Service?" *American Prospect*, Summer 1995, pp. 14–17. A most hyperbolic attack is Michael Gartner, "Give Me Old Time Journalism," *Quill*, November/December 1995, pp. 66–69.

2. Max Frankel, "Fix-It Journalism," *New York Times Magazine*, May 20, 1995, p. 30.

3. Richard Harwood, "Civic Journalism 101," *Washington Post*, January 17, 1995, p. A22. For a response to Harwood's skeptical treatment, see Joann Byrd, "Conversations with the Community," *Washington Post*, February 5, 1995, p. C6.

4. Quoted in Glaberson, "A New Press Role."

5. Frankel, "Fix-It Journalism," p. 28.

6. Michael Kelly, "David Gergen: Master of the Game," *New York Times Magazine*, October 31, 1993, pp. 94, 97.

7. Harry Rosenfeld, "We Regret to Report that Civic Journalism Is a Bad Idea," *Times-Union*, October 1, 1995, p. 15.

8. Quoted in Michael Hoyt, "Are You Now, or Will You Ever Be, a Civic Journalist?" *Columbia Journalism Review*, September/October 1995, p. 29.

See William F. Woo, "As Old Gods Falter: Public Journalism and the Tradition of Detachment," Press Enterprise Lecture no. 30, University of California-Riverside, February 13, 1995.

9. Quoted in Case, "Public Journalism Denounced," p. 15.

10. For a useful discussion of this approach, popular with many in public journalism, see The Harwood Group, *Meaningful Chaos: How People Form Relationships with Public Concerns* (Dayton: Kettering Foundation, 1993).

11. Cole Campbell, remarks to James K. Batten Symposium of Civic Journalism, sponsored by the Pew Center for Civic Journalism, Washington, D.C., September 13, 1995.

CHAPTER 3

1. On the decline in readership and the efforts to combat it, see Susan Miller, "America's Dailies and the Drive to Capture Lost Readers," *Gannett Center Journal* 1, no. 1 (Spring 1987): 56–68; Leo Bogart, *Preserving the Press: How Daily Newspapers Mobilized to Keep Readers* (New York: Columbia University Press, 1991); Richard O'Mara, "The Flight from Newspapers," *Quill*, March 1990, pp. 34–37; Howard Kurtz, "Yesterday's News: Why Newspapers Are Losing Their Franchise," in Frank Denton and Howard Kurtz, *Reinventing the Newspaper* (New York: Twentieth Century Fund Press, 1993); Howard Kurtz, *Media Circus: The Trouble with America's Newspapers* (New York: Times Books, 1993), chapter 15.

2. Report from Times Mirror Center for the People and the Press, Washington, D.C., April 6, 1995, pp. 9, 29.

3. See Doug Underwood, *When MBAs Rule the Newsroom* (New York: Columbia University Press, 1993); James D. Squires, *Read All About It: The Corporate Takeover of America's Newspapers* (New York: Times Books, 1993); Alison Carper, "Paint-By-Numbers Journalism: How Reader Surveys and Focus Groups Subvert a Democratic Press," paper published by the Joan Shorenstein Center on Press, Politics and Public Policy, Harvard University, April 1995. For a contrasting view see Frank Denton, "Old Newspapers and New Realities: The Promise of the Marketing of Journalism," in Denton and Kurtz, *Reinventing the Newspaper.*

4. Philip Meyer, "An Ethic for the Information Age," in L. Hodges, ed., *Social Responsibility: Business, Journalism, Law, Medicine* (Lexington, Va.: Washington and Lee University, 1990, pp. 14–21).

5. Ibid., p. 15.

6. See Kurtz, "Yesterday's News," pp. 62–63.

7. Quoted in Underwood, *When MBAs Rule the Newsroom,* p. 14.

8. Quoted in Mark Jurkowitz, "Endangered Species," *Boston Phoenix,* December 31, 1993, p. 22.

9. For a good overview of the range of concerns, see two special sections in the publications of the Nieman Foundation, "Can Journalism Shape the New Technologies?" *Nieman Reports* 68, no. 2 (Summer 1994); and "Running Scared Into the On-Line Era," *Nieman Reports* 69, no. 2 (Summer 1995). A more

optimistic statement is Max Frankel, "Horseless in Cyberspace," *New York Times Magazine*, May 14, 1995, p. 18. For a sweeping treatment by the nation's leading journalism scholar, see James W. Carey, "The Press, Public Opinion and Public Discourse," in Theodorde L. Glasser and Charles T. Salmon, eds., *Public Opinion and Communication of Consent* (New York: Guilford Press, 1995).

10. Bill Kovach, "Who's Going to Make the Decisions? Who's Going to Set the Values?" *Nieman Reports* 68, no. 2 (Summer 1994): 4.

11. Bill Kovach, "Protecting Values in the New Era," *Nieman Reports* 69, no. 2 (Summer 1995): 2.

12. The literature on the faltering of political journalism is voluminous. Some of the more arresting works are Robert Entman, *Democracy without Citizens: Media and the Decay of American Politics* (New York: Oxford University Press, 1989); Kiku Adatto, "Sound Bite Democracy: Network Evening News Presidential Campaign Coverage, 1968 and 1988," Joan Shorenstein Center on Press, Politics and Public Policy, Harvard University, June 1990; Todd Gitlin, "Blips, Bites and Savvy Talk," *Dissent*, Winter 1990, pp. 18–26; Larry J. Sabato, *Feeding Frenzy: How Attack Journalism Has Transformed American Politics* (New York: Free Press, 1991); Kathleen Hall Jamieson, *Dirty Politics: Deception, Distraction, and Democracy* (New York: Oxford University Press, 1992); Thomas E. Patterson, *Out of Order* (New York: Knopf, 1993). These are all scholarly accounts. For views from a journalist on the same problems, see Tom Rosenstiel, *Strange Bedfellows: How Television and the Presidential Candidates Changed American Politics*, 1992 (New York: Hyperion, 1992); Tom Rosenstiel, *The Beat Goes On: President Clinton's First Year with the Media* (New York: Twentieth Century Fund Press, 1994). For the author's own treatment of the subject, see Jay Rosen, "Politics, Vision, and the Press," in Jay Rosen and Paul Taylor, *The New News v. the Old News: The Press and Politics in the 1990s* (New York: Twentieth Century Fund Press, 1992); Jay Rosen, "No Content: The Press, Politics and Public Philosophy," *Tikkun*, May/June 1992, pp. 11–14, 77–80; Jay Rosen, "Who Won the Week?" *Tikkun*, July/August 1993, pp. 7–10, 94.

13. See Jon Katz, "Rock, Rap and Movies Bring You the News," *Rolling Stone*, March 5, 1992, p. 35–38; Paul Taylor, "Political Coverage in the 1990s: Teaching the Old News New Tricks," in Rosen and Taylor, *The New News v. the Old News*; Ellen Hume, "Tabloids, Talk Radio and the Future of News: Technology's Impact on Journalism," The Annenberg Washington Program, Washington, D.C., 1995.

14. *Yankelovich Monitor 1994: Managing Change in the 1990s*, Yankelovich Partners, New York, February 1994, p. 22.

15. G. Cleveland Wilhoit and David Weaver, "U.S. Journalists at Work, 1971–1992," paper presented to the annual convention of the Association for Education in Journalism and Mass Communication, Atlanta, August 10–13, 1994, p. 41, table 8.

16. On the depressed atmosphere in newsrooms, see Underwood, *When MBAs Rule the Newsroom*, chapters 3, 10, and 12; Sheryl and Pete Danko,

"Kissing the Newsroom Goodbye," *American Journalism Review*, June 1995, pp. 30–35, 43; Carl Sessions Stepp, "The Thrill Is Gone," *American Journalism Review*, October 1995, pp. 15–19.

17. Stepp, "The Thrill Is Gone," p. 15; *A Call to Leadership*, Poynter Institute for Media Studies, St. Petersburg, Fla., 1992, p. 1.

18. For an indication of the ranges of concerns, see the special section, "Ethics on Trial," in *Nieman Reports* 68, no. 1 (Spring 1994); Beverly Kees and Bill Phillips, *Nothing Sacred: Journalism, Politics and Public Trust in a Tell-All Age*, Freedom Forum First Amendment Center at Vanderbilt University, 1994.

19. Sabato, *Feeding Frenzy*, p. 222.

20. Quoted in Kees and Phillips, *Nothing Sacred*, p. 38.

21. Weston Kosova, "Washington Diarist," *New Republic*, April 18, 1994, p. 50.

22. Rosenstiel, *Beat Goes On*, p. 3.

23. On the press and its search for the hidden motive, see James W. Carey, "The Dark Continent of American Journalism," in Robert Karl Manoff and Michael Schudson, eds., *Reading the News* (New York: Pantheon, 1986), pp. 146–96.

24. Quoted in Paul Starobin, "A Generation of Vipers: Journalists and the New Cynicism," *Columbia Journalism Review*, March/April 1995, p. 29. See also William Glaberson, "The New Press Criticism: News as the Enemy of Hope," *New York Times*, October 9, 1994, section IV, p. 1; David S. Broder, "War on Cynicism," *Washington Post*, July 6, 1994, p. A18.

25. See, for example, Meg Greenfield, "The Cynicism Complaint," *Newsweek*, September 12, 1994. Also relevant are the letters in reply to Starobin's article "A Generation of Vipers" in *Columbia Journalism Review*, July/August 1995, pp. 6–7.

26. Paul Taylor, *See How They Run: Electing the President in an Age of Mediaocracy* (New York: Knopf, 1990), p. 255.

27. Katharine Q. Seelye, "Wouldn't Mother Have Been Proud?" *New York Times*, June 18, 1995, section IV, p. 5.

28. Howard Kurtz, "Tuning Out Traditional News," *Washington Post*, May 23, 1995, p. A1.

29. Quoted in Thomas B. Rosenstiel, "Reporters Putting Their Own Spin on News Events," *Los Angeles Times*, November 25, 1993, pp. A1, 17–18.

30. R. W. Apple, "A Deflated Presidency," *New York Times*, January 25, 1995, p. A1.

31. Tony Wharton, "State of the Union Reaction," *Virginian-Pilot*, January 26, 1995, p. A1.

32. See Thomas E. Patterson, *Out of Order* (New York: Knopf, 1993), especially pp. 57–91; Rosenstiel, *The Beat Goes On*.

33. On objectivity in journalism see Michael Schudson, *Discovering the News: A Social History of American Newspapers* (New York: Basic Books, 1978); Theodore Glasser, "Objectivity Precludes Responsibility," *Quill*, February 1984, pp. 13–16; Jay Rosen, "Beyond Objectivity," *Nieman Reports* 67, no. 4 (Winter 1993): 48–53.

34. Bill Kovach, "Moving Beyond Cold War Journalism," unpublished manuscript, 1992, p. 14.

35. Tom Rosenstiel reported on a study of 1,300 news stories on the front page of the *New York Times, Washington Post*, and *Los Angeles Times* during

two-month period in 1993: 51 percent could be classified as "news"; 5 percent were "features"; 5 percent were "special projects"; 40 percent were "analytical" or "interpretive" treatments. Of this 40 percent, four out of five were not labeled "analysis" or something similar. See Rosenstiel, "Reporters Putting Their Own Spin on News Events."

36. Squires, *Read All About It*, pp. 139, 169. For further evidence in support of this view, see Underwood, *When MBAs Rule the Newsroom*.

37. Nieman Foundation, "Can Journalism Shape the New Technologies?" p. 54.

38. Marvin Kalb, "The State of the Disunion," *New York Times*, February 4, 1995, p. 27. See also Patterson, *Out of Order*, pp. 88–89; David Broder, "A New Assignment for the Press," Press Enterprise Lecture no. 26, University of California-Riverside, February 12, 1991.

CHAPTER 4

1. See James K. Batten, "Newspapers and Communities," in Jay Rosen, *Community-Connectedness: Passwords for Public Journalism*, Poynter Institute for Media Studies, St. Petersburg, Fla., 1993, p. 14.

2. Davis Merritt, Jr., "A New Political Contract: Must Restore Meaning to Election Campaigns," *Wichita Eagle*, November 13, 1988, p. 3B.

3. Davis Merritt, Jr., "Up Front, Here's Our Election Bias," *Wichita Eagle*, September 9, 1990, p. 13A.

4. For an example of such an analysis, see William Safire, "The Double Wedge," *New York Times*, February 23, 1995, p. A23.

5. This description is adapted from Steve Smith, "Your Vote Counts: The Wichita Eagle's Election Project," *National Civic Review*, Summer 1991, pp. 24–30; Davis Merritt, Jr., *Public Journalism and Public Life: Why Telling the News Is Not Enough* (Hillsdale, N.J.: Lawrence Erlbaum Associates, 1995), chapter 7. See also Michael Hoyt, "The Wichita Experiment," *Columbia Journalism Review*, July/August 1992, pp. 43–47; John Bare, "Case Study—Wichita and Charlotte: The Leap of a Passive Press to Activism," *Media Studies Journal* 6, no. 4 (Fall 1992): 149–60.

6. *Wichita Eagle*, October 7, 1990, pp. 1D, 2D.

7. On the adversarial pose, see Adam Gopnik's analysis of journalism's "culture of aggression" in his "Read All About It," *New Yorker*, December 12, 1994, pp. 84, 86–90, 92–94, 96, 98–102. On the limitations of "balance," see Merritt, *Public Journalism and Public Life*, pp. 19–20.

8. Merritt, *Public Journalism and Public Life*, p. 82.

9. This description is adapted from the *Wichita Eagle*'s special reprint, "Solving It Ourselves: The People Project," *Wichita Eagle* and Beacon Publishing Company, Wichita, 1992; Merritt, *Public Journalism and Public Life*, pp. 84–86; various internal planning memos provided to the author by Merritt.

10. E. J. Dionne, *Why Americans Hate Politics* (New York: Simon and Schuster, 1991), p. 354.

11. Merritt, *Public Journalism and Public Life*, p. 86.

12. Ibid., p. 83.

13. This description is developed from Edward D. Miller, *The Charlotte Project: Helping Citizens Take Back Democracy* (St. Petersburg, Fla.: Poynter Institute for Media Studies, 1994). See also Bare, "Case Study—Wichita and Charlotte," pp. 149–60.

14. Rich Oppel, "We'll Help You Regain Control of the Issues," *Charlotte Observer*, January 12, 1992, p. A1. See David Broder, "Democracy and the Press," *Washington Post*, January 3, 1990, p. A15; David Broder, "A New Assignment for the Press," Press Enterprise Lecture no. 26, University of California-Riverside, February 12, 1991, p. 12.

15. Michael Schudson, *The Power of News* (Cambridge, Mass.: Harvard University Press, 1995), p. 25.

16. Miller, *Charlotte Project*, pp. 65–67.

17. Ibid., p. 16.

18. Oppel's remarks are from the transcript of the Project on Public Life and the Press fall seminar at American Press Institute, Reston, Va., November 10–12, 1993, p. 117, available from the Kettering Foundation, Dayton.

19. Thomas E. Patterson, *Out of Order* (New York: Knopf, 1993), pp. 55–56.

20. "Readers' Questions for Bush; Some Answered," *Charlotte Observer*, July 5, 1992, p. A2.

CHAPTER 5

1. David Mathews, *Politics for People: Finding a Responsible Public Voice* (Urbana, Ill.: University of Illinois Press, 1994), pp. 3, 40.

2. For a fuller description of the Project's origins see Jay Rosen, "Making Things More Public: On the Political Responsibility of the Media Intellectual," *Critical Studies in Mass Communication* 11, no. 4 (December 1994): 363–88.

3. Tom Still, "News Organizations Must Become Campaign Players," *Wisconsin State Journal*, February 22, 1995, p. A15.

4. This description is based on the author's personal interview with Still, July 18, 1995. See also Frank Denton and Esther Thorson, *Civic Journalism: Does it Work?*, Pew Center for Civic Journalism, Washington, D.C., 1995; *Civic Journalism: Six Case Studies*, Pew Center for Civic Journalism, Washington, D.C., 1995.

5. "Ratings: A Runaway Winner," *Civic Catalyst*, Pew Center for Civic Journalism, Washington, D.C., October 1995, p. 11.

6. This description is based on the author's personal interview with John Dinges, July 20, 1995.

7. "Democracy and Citizenship: Creating New Conversations," *Virginian-Pilot*, April 9, 1995, p. A1.

8. "Democracy and Citizenship: Creating New Conversations," *Virginian-Pilot*, April 16, 1995, p. A1.

9. "Democracy and Citizenship: Creating New Conversations," *Virginian-Pilot*, April 23, 1995, p. J1.

10. Quotations are from the author's personal interview with Hartig, July 11, 1995.

11. Paul Taylor, *See How They Run: Electing the President in an Age of Mediaocracy* (New York: Knopf, 1990), p. 23.

12. Cole C. Campbell, "We Must Discuss Issues to Ensure a Stronger, Less Divisive Society," *Virginian-Pilot*, April 9, 1995, p. A2.

CHAPTER 6

1. Jane R. Eisner, "Should Journalists Abandon Their Detachment to Solve Problems?" *Philadelphia Inquirer*, October 16, 1994, p. E7. Italics in original.

2. Davis Merritt, Jr., *Public Journalism and Public Life: Why Telling the News Is Not Enough* (Hillsdale, N.J.: Lawrence Erlbaum Associates, 1995), pp. 93–94.

3. This description is based on the author's interview with Randy Hammer, July 19, 1995, and on the special section, "Our Jobs, Our Children, Our Future," *Herald-Dispatch*, November 19, 1993, pp. E1–12.

4. Hodding Carter III, "If You Can't Do Both, Get Out of the Business," *Civic Catalyst*, Pew Center for Civic Journalism, Washington, D.C., October 1995, pp. 10–11.

CHAPTER 7

1. Davis Merritt, Jr., *Public Journalism and Public Life: Why Telling the News Is Not Enough* (Hillsdale, N.J.: Lawrence Erlbaum Associates, 1995), p. 6.

2. Phyllis Kaniss, *The Media and the Mayor's Race: The Failure of Urban Political Reporting* (Bloomington, Ind.: Indiana University Press, 1995), p. 21.

3. Ibid., p. 23.

4. Quoted in "The Real Public Journalism," *American Journalism Review*, January/February 1995, p. 25.

5. See Cole Campbell, "League Takes Us at Our Word, Studies Our Effort to Serve Citizens Better," *Virginian-Pilot*, June 18, 1995, p. A2.

CHAPTER 8

1. Osborn Elliott, "Time for the Press to Get Involved," John Hersey Memorial Lecture, Key West, Fla., January 12, 1995, p. 23.

2. David Broder, "Democracy and the Press," *Washington Post*, January 3, 1990, p. A15.

3. Max Frankel, "Horseless in Cyberspace," *New York Times Magazine*, May 13, 1995, p. 18.

4. Max Frankel, "Fix-It Journalism," *New York Times Magazine*, May 20, 1995, p. 28.

5. Davis Merritt, "Public Journalism: Defining a Democratic Art," *Media Studies Journal* 9, no. 3 (Summer 1995): 131.

6. Quoted in Mark Jurkowitz, "Reforming the Media," *Boston Globe Magazine*, July 9, 1995, p. 22.

7. Author's interview with Tom Hamburger, July 25, 1995.

8. Tom Hamburger, "The Minnesota Compact," *Star Tribune*, June 23, 1995, p. 16A. See also E. J. Dionne, "The Minnesota Compact," *Washington Post*, July 13, 1995, p. A17.

9. Author's interview with Tom Hamburger, July 25, 1995.

10. The "Voters Voice Mission Statement" was issued originally by New Hampshire Public Television, New Hampshire Public Radio, WGOT News , *The Telegraph* (Nashua), and the *Portsmouth Herald*.

11. Max Jennings, editor of the *Dayton Daily News*, told readers in July 1995 that his newspaper "is going to continue its public journalism approach, as will many others." He wrote, "Others will continue along more traditional channels—what we call 'boys on the bus' reporting. . . . In this version of election coverage, the candidates will set the themes and make the speeches and be covered as warranted. In the public journalism version we'll practice, we intend to let our readers, not the candidates, determine what the issues are. Then we intend to get the candidates to respond to the readers' concerns instead of what they might prefer to discuss." Max Jennings, "We're Looking for Ways to Connect," *Dayton Daily News*, July 9, 1995, p. 88.

CHAPTER 9

1. David Broder, "A New Assignment for the Press," Press Enterprise Lecture no. 26, The Press Enterprise, Riverside, Calif., 1991, p. 5.

2. Leonard Downie, Jr., "News and Opinion at the Post," *Washington Post Weekly Edition*, October 18, 1992, p. 7 (italics added).

3. Quoted in *Civic Catalyst*, Pew Center for Civic Journalism, Washington, D.C., October 1995, p. 6.

4. James W. Carey, "A Republic, If You Can Keep It: Liberty and Public Life in the Age of Glasnost," in Raymond Arsenault, *Crucible of Liberty: 200 Years of the Bill of Rights* (New York: Free Press, 1991), pp. 118, 128.

CHAPTER 10

1. Jean Bethke Elshtain, *Democracy on Trial* (New York: Basic Books, 1994), p. 5.

2. Hannah Arendt, *Essays in Understanding* (New York: Harcourt Brace, 1994), p. 323.

INDEX

About the Author

J ay Rosen is an associate professor of journalism at New York University and director of the Project on Public Life and the Press. He is also an associate of the Kettering Foundation. Since 1993 he has been identified with the reform movement known as public journalism, on which he has written and lectured widely. His writings have appeared in *Harpers*, the *Nation*, the *Los Angeles Times*, *Tikkun*, and many other journals. He is presently completing a book on public journalism to be published in 1997 by Yale University Press.